D1269285

JEAN SIBELIUS
A Master and His Work

JEAN SIBELIUS

A Master and His Work

By NILS-ERIC RINGBOM

Translated from the Swedish by G. I. C. de Courcy

UNIVERSITY OF OKLAHOMA PRESS

NORMAN

Library of Congress Catalog Card Number: 54–10061

Copyright 1954 in the United States by the University of Oklahoma Press, Publishing Division of the University. Composed and printed at Norman, Oklahoma, U.S.A., by the University of Oklahoma Press.
First American edition.

Preface

My purpose in this book has been to present a biography
of Jean Sibelius combined with a general survey and
analysis of his stylistic development. For those already
familiar with the earlier exhaustive works of Erik Furuhjelm and Karl Ekman—upon which the biographical
portions of my study are largely based—I do not claim to
have presented any essentially new facts concerning the
external life and the personality of the composer. But
in setting forth in concise form the distinctive features
and qualities of his principal compositions and his highly
individualistic style, I have proceeded independently,
finding new approaches and correcting previous mis-
understandings. In order to keep the text agreeably free
of footnotes, I have refrained, in the interest of the general reader, from identifying the various authorities
quoted in the progress of the work. Their names will be
clear from the context. Wherever, for stylistic reasons,
the source of Sibelius' quoted statements is not expressly
indicated, these derive either from Ekman's work or my
own conversations with the composer. Other source
material is listed in the bibliography.

I wish to take this opportunity of expressing to Professor Jean Sibelius my deep gratitude for the kindness
and courtesy shown me during the preparation of this

work and for the appreciation and sympathy he has manifested for my personal points of view.

Nils-Eric Ringbom

Helsinki, 1948

Contents

	Preface	*v*
I	Apprenticeship of a Nature Lover	3
II	Inspirations from the Kalevala	29
III	At the Turn of the Century	53
IV	At the Turning Point	79
V	*Voces intimae*	97
VI	Impressionistic Harmonies	117
VII	Three Symphonies and a Suite Champêtre	132
VIII	*Negotium cum dignitate*	158
	Complete List of Works	163
	Bibliography	186
	Index	188

Illustrations

Four Portraits of Jean Sibelius:

    in 1889, 1915, 1935, and 1953   *facing page* 22

A Page from the First

    Manuscript of the First Symphony   54

In the Studio of Wäinö Aaltonen, 1935   102

Sibelius in His Garden, 1947   102

Villa Ainola   102

Jean Sibelius and Sir Thomas Beecham, 1954   150

JEAN SIBELIUS
A Master and His Work

I

Apprenticeship of a Nature Lover

J_{ean} *Sibelius* occupies a unique position in the music of our time. Over thirty years ago the Danish musicologist Gunnar Hauch voiced, with admirable sagacity, the opinion that Sibelius was *the* great personality in an arid period when the last giants in the history of music were still casting their shadows over their descendants— *the* great personality in an interregnum when those who aspired to fame and influence either clung anxiously to old rules and traditions or tried by every possible means to arouse interest in a music that possessed only the negative qualities of the "new."

Sibelius kept aloof from all such things. His art also represents something altogether new in the history of music—not "new" just for the sake of it, but because a genial artist cannot help creating something new if he follows the laws of his own nature. Sibelius went his own way, and even if at first the paths he trod seemed to many dark and obscure, when viewed as a whole they admittedly led to lofty goals, which he pursued with indomitable energy. He has never been content to rest on his laurels but has striven constantly to advance, and this aspiration, this perpetual flight from the stereotyped and the conventional has become part of his being and a hallmark of his music.

Jean (Johan) Julius Christian Sibelius was born on December 8, 1865, at Tavastehus in the interior of Finland. His family and friends called him by the pet name Janne (Johnnie), but Jean was the name by which he was to be known in the outside world. His parents were Christian Gustaf Sibelius (a doctor and surgeon) and Maria Charlotta Sibelius, *née* Borg. The family name was derived from *Sibbe,* a farm in East Nyland belonging to his great-grandfather who towards the middle of the eighteenth century moved from the Finnish hinterland to the coast district settled by Swedish-speaking Finns. Thus his descendants were Swedish by language and customs, Janne's grandfather, Johann Sibelius (town councilor in Lovisa) also having married the daughter of a doctor who had immigrated from Sweden. On his mother's side, Sibelius descended from a family of soldiers, government officials, and clergymen in which Finnish and Swedish blood had intermingled for many centuries.

The question whether he is predominantly Finnish or Swedish has never interested him in the least. "Though stemming from families whose language and culture had been Swedish for many generations [wrote Ekman], he allied himself enthusiastically with the national Finnish movement in an agitated period of patriotic revival, and with the unerring instinct of genius was able—besides the superabundant multiplicity of new expressive values he gave the world of music—to express in his own music as genuine and convincing national Finnish feelings and ideals as if they had sprung directly from the depths of the Finnish soul. This faculty of entering wholeheartedly into the spirit of Finnish national thought and feeling has been wedded freely to the natural respect of a distinguished personality for the binding sanctity of childhood's memories and racial traditions."

Sibelius' description of his childhood environment shows clearly that his musical talent was a heritage from both his father and his mother, even though as far as we know none of his ancestors ever followed music as a profession. Having lost their father in their very early youth, the three children—Linda, the eldest, Janne, and his brother Christian, who was three years his junior—clung all the more fervently to their mother. "She had a gentle, very feminine nature [Sibelius told Ekman]. Very reserved in manner, she captivated all who came to know her better by her naturalness, her even, harmonious nature, and her love of mankind."

Today Tavastehus is still a smallish country town, and in 1860 it was even smaller and more idyllic, but it had a rich cultural life fostered by the landowners, officials, and teachers in the district, though there were no industries in the town and it was neither a commercial nor a business center of any importance. One alien element at that time, as Sibelius tells us, was the Russian garrison which had been transferred to Tavastehus after the Finnish battalions were disbanded. The Russian officers and their families brought with them a breath of the great world, and like the cultivated families of the town were keenly interested in music and attended the local concerts, which were given by the small orchestras from Helsinki[1] and Turku, choirs from different places, and the country's finest singers.

[1]*Swedish*	*Finnish*
Helsingfors	Helsinki
Tavastehus	Hämeenlinna
Åbo	Turku

Sibelius had in every respect a happy, harmonious childhood. He was no infant prodigy and grew up with all the manifold hobbies, inclinations, and naughtinesses of any normal youngster, though he seems to have been more introspective and sensitive than boys in general. At the age of five he showed his musical aptitude by composing little harmonies and melodies on the piano and from his ninth year received systematic instruction on the piano, but scales and finger exercises did not interest him very greatly; so that his progress was anything but brilliant. He much preferred to lose himself "in free improvisations." The violin appealed to him far more.

"When I was about fifteen years old [he said] music took such hold of me that it soon drove all other interests from my mind. I then began to study the violin with Gustav Levander, the military bandmaster and the best teacher of that instrument in my native town. I was completely carried away with it. For the next ten years my dearest wish, my proudest ambition, was to be a great violin virtuoso."

The thing that distinguished him so greatly from other children was his really passionate love of nature, which occupied his thoughts to the exclusion of everything else. Expeditions through the woods and fields and excursions on the lakes meant far more to him than the conventional diversions and recreations. The family used to spend the summer in the islands off the coast of Lovisa or in Sääksmäki in the province of Tavastland.

"Janne was a great dreamer [wrote his boyhood friend, Walter von Konow]. He had a lively imagination and reacted quickly to external impressions. It drew rich nourishment from his intense love of nature. He was fond of making long excursions in the vicinity of Tavastehus

6

and through the woods at Sääksmäki. His imagination gave life to everything round him. In the dusk of evening he enjoyed hunting for fairies in the darkest corners of the woods, and if his fancy ever happened to take a macabre turn, roving about with him through the dark woods peopled by trolls and witches and other weird creatures could give one quite a creepy sensation. Beautiful sunsets brought out another side of his fantasy. We would sit for hours gazing in silent wonder at the setting sun in the midst of shimmering gold and purple clouds, and then a whole world of faery, enchanting and beautiful, revealed itself to us."

But this dreamer and visionary fortunately also had a very strong sense of reality, which increased as he grew older and kept an overstrung imagination from getting the upper hand, letting the bewitching world of faery give place to a healthy intercourse with nature. The study of nature in all its forms was also the principal interest of the growing boy. He was a passionate collector of plants and insects, and his herbarium was the best in his class, but otherwise he was anything but a model pupil. "He found it difficult to sit still during lessons and listen to things that did not interest him [continued von Konow, who was his classmate in the Finnish normal school in Tavastehus]. He would sit lost in thought and was quite faraway if he were suddenly asked a question. He took little interest in homework, but he was an omnivorous reader of books other than his text books—not only books for boys, but the works of good authors; and when he grew older he was greatly interested in historical works"—a taste that he has retained down to the present day.

His musical gifts developed harmoniously with his

7

other natural aptitudes. He very largely taught himself the rudiments, although he was guided from time to time by relatives or a regular teacher. However, he neither applied himself very industriously to his piano lessons nor, as already mentioned, did he make any notable progress. "I was only interested in free improvisations," he said.

At the age of ten he wrote his first composition, a little piece for violin and cello *pizzicato* entitled *Waterdrops*. Erik Furuhjelm, who published the opening bars of this little tone poem in his work on the composer, wrote that the "little song in three-part form manifested an instinctive feeling for form" and that here, as in everything that Sibelius wrote when he was a boy, "he did not follow the traditional scheme in which the third section coincides in all respects with the first, but introduced a little surprise at the end. Even at that age he seems to have avoided instinctively an empty, schematic repetition and tried to spin out his modest little theme further." He displayed much more industry and took greater interest in his study of the violin, and the regular instruction he received for five years from the military bandmaster soon enabled him to appear as violin soloist at school festivals and other such occasions. In addition —which was far more important for his development— he began to take part in chamber-music ensembles with his brother and sister who were likewise studying music. The three now formed a family trio with Janne as violinist and soul of the group, his sister Linda at the piano, and his brother Christian (later a physician and professor of psychiatry) playing the cello. Besides making music at home, Janne also played in the private quartets of different families who cultivated chamber music.

In this way, he acquired very early a deep knowledge of stringed instruments and an extensive acquaintance with chamber-music literature, especially the classics. This drew his attention more and more to the formal, instrumental aspect of a musical work, which stimulated his own productivity. Chancing to run across a copy of Marx's *Kompositionslehre* in the school library, he studied it assiduously from then on, which (as he says) gave him such a comprehensive idea of musical form that when he began to study music seriously in Helsinki five years later, he "already knew practically everything he had to know."

Quite naturally his creative gift first expressed itself in the field of chamber music. The fragments of a trio in A minor and a piano quartet in E minor, which still survive in manuscript, follow classical models, although some of the emotional parts seem to have been inspired by the romanticism of the early nineteenth century.

But more noteworthy than these unoriginal attempts is a cycle for piano and violin (Suite in D minor) consisting of a couple of elegiac tone poems that break away quite suddenly and abruptly from the folk rhythms. In addition to greater technical assurance, the suite contains lyrical ideas of a bright, northern coloring with fresh, robust accents. It has been asserted that Grieg was very obviously the sponsor of many things in this composition, but it manifests at the same time little melodic and rhythmical traits that already reveal the emerging contour of an independent artistic individuality. The opening bars of an *andantino* in C Major for piano and cello, dating from 1884, are also anything but conventional, and further on there is a crescendo effect of distinctly personal character.

With Sibelius the creative urge sprang from a musical environment and an intimate contact with nature. He worked intensively at his technical training as a violinist and creative artist, without making any attempt to force it. But it was primarily nature that remained his source of inspiration. "I loved to take my violin along on my summer rambles [he said] so that whenever I felt inspired I could express it in music. In Kalalahti (while we were summering in Sääkmäki) I sought out, as a platform, a large stone with an entrancingly lovely view of Lake Vanajavesi and here I gave endless concerts for the birds. The outskirts of Lovisa were just as great an inspiration. When sailing I often stood in the bow with my violin and improvised something to the sea."

Even during his school days he became more and more wrapped up in his music and his adoration of the beauties of nature, not only in its summer aspects but also in those peculiar to the neighborhood of his birthplace. His school tasks naturally did not gain thereby. Still, though school had little attraction for him, he had to go through with it nonetheless, for at that time, more than today, far greater weight was laid on a leaving examination. This was considered an imperative duty of the sons of good families, and Sibelius' family was evidently horrified at the idea that the lad would not finish his schooling in the traditional way. His diligent application to his musical studies was responsible for his failure to pass his fifth-grade examinations, but from then on things went better, and in the spring of 1885 he successfully passed his final examinations.

He had now escaped from the restraints of school and the necessity of studying all sorts of subjects that did not interest him in the least, but this by no means ended the toil and trouble of acquiring an education. One way or another he still "had to make something of himself," so he embarked on a course of jurisprudence at the University in Helsinki. "My grandmother would never have understood if I had chosen such a dubious and far from respected career as that of a musician [he said]. She naturally appreciated my musical talents and was very proud of my efforts at composition but the mere thought of music as a profession simply horrified her. In view of what she had meant to my mother and to us children since my father's death, I naturally tried as long as I could to avoid causing her disappointment."

If he had now satisfied what his family considered their reasonable demands by entering the university, he still did not feel in duty bound to forswear his further musical education. So he at once enrolled as a special student at the Academy of Music, where he studied violin and musical theory. He made no progress with his legal studies, and one day when one of his maternal uncles came to see him during a visit to the capital and discovered an open text book, the pages of which had yellowed from long exposure to the spring sun, he and the rest of the family realized that it was wiser to let Janne go his own way.

He took violin lessons from Csillag, a temperamental Hungarian on the teaching staff of the Academy of Music, and studied theory with the founder and director, Martin Wegelius. In the beginning he looked upon the theoretical studies merely as a complement to his violin playing, which interested him far more. "From my fifteenth year [he said] I played the violin almost continually from morning to night for ten long years. I detested pen and ink; and much preferred an elegant bow. My predilection for the violin lasted a long time and it was a very painful awakening to discover that I had begun my study too late for the arduous career of a virtuoso. I was at the age when one chases chimeras and avoids looking reality in the face until the very last minute." Nevertheless he carried it so far that while a student at the Academy he was able to play an exacting work like Mendelssohn's concerto and was appointed second fiddle in the school's string quartet, the other three members of which were on the teaching staff.

Wegelius had the young musical adept begin with the elementary subjects—general musical theory and thorough bass. Next came harmony, strict and free polyphony, and form based on Bussler's *Practical School of Composition,* which led gradually from the strict ecclesiastical style of the Middle Ages to the free style of the nineteenth century. "Martin Wegelius was always a fatherly friend to me [Sibelius told Ekman]. His interest was not confined to what I did as a pupil within the walls of the Academy. It went much farther than that, which was all the more remarkable seeing that with his neoromantic leanings he could not agree with me on all points, though before strangers he always sang my praises." As a teacher Wegelius was of a "dictatorial nature, extremely anxious that a pupil should hold strictly to the scheduled program. He would at times get very angry if his instructions were not obeyed to the letter."

If we disregard the impersonal, technically correct works of the student that were the direct product of Wegelius' teaching, it is principally the F Major Sonata for violin and piano (written in the winter 1886–87) that deserves attention. Here the easy unaffected treatment of the form and the mature chordal (vertical) structure represent a very striking departure from traditional canons. If we seek a model for this sonata, it will be found that the building of subjects, the key distribution and the whole layout of the work bear a close relationship to Grieg's sonata in the same key. It is quite obvious that the Norwegian composer's lyrical work was the inspiration for Sibelius' composition and to a certain extent the model also. Sibelius himself has admitted that during the first half of the eighties he was very strongly influenced by Grieg. Nevertheless there are parts of the sonata that are unmistakably original, and there can be no question of a direct imitation of the Norwegian artist. "None of it is secondhand art [said Furuhjelm]. Most of it has been personally experienced and the specific coloring stems from the environment. Sibelius imparted no Norwegian nuances to the landscape whose beauty had enraptured him."

After three years of study, during which he had dutifully carried out Wegelius' program—although without manifesting much enthusiasm for it—his teacher saw that it was now time to give his pupil a little freer rein and allow him, even in the work in his regular course of study, to develop the individual style that he had already manifested in his independent compositions. The fruits of this were the two works with which he concluded his studies at the academy: a string trio in A Major and a string quartet in A minor, both performed in the spring of 1889. These works marked his real debut as a composer and displayed an originality of technique and invention that astounded the leading musicians of the Finnish capital. Karl Flodin of the *Nya Pressen*—the leading critic in the country—found that the five movements of the string suite "bore evidence that their creator had studied intelligently the tonal secrets of the string quartet and had taken a real part in their production. The independent contrapuntal treatment of the three instruments was also first rate—inspired in fact; not excellent in the usual scholastic sense, but thoroughly new and modern. I was frankly impressed by this composer's debut."

His verdict on the A minor quartet was no less enthusiastic. "In this composition, Sibelius has given such brilliant proof of his original musical talent that we may expect the greatest things of him. In all the different movements of the quartet one finds a wealth of ideas and an independence combined with complete mastery of technical difficulties—qualities that in such a young composer must be considered really unique." It is interesting to compare these remarks with Flodin's harsh judgment of the young maestro when he really showed the claws of the lion in his Kalevala Legend.

Among Sibelius' friends at the academy, Ferruccio Busoni—who taught piano there in 1888–89—holds a special place. Without doubt he was also the most distinguished of the eminent foreign teachers that Wegelius succeeded in capturing for his little music school. It is said that the aforementioned string trio opened Busoni's eyes to Sibelius' unique gifts, and twenty-five years later (1916) he confirmed this opinion when he performed Sibelius' Second Symphony in Zürich and published a short article in the daily press by way of introduction. This friendship was of great importance for Sibelius, although the two men were opposites in more ways than one. Busoni grew up as a boy prodigy, and from his earliest childhood had lived in the hotels of large European cities, coming into contact with nature for the first time during his residence in Finland. "In the early stages of our friendship [said Sibelius] he could never get over how much I had gained through my contact with nature. Later he understood me better, although with his very pronounced intellectual, reflective attitude he could never surrender himself directly to nature's impressions." But long after this meeting in their youth, Sibelius was to learn that Busoni's friendship and regard for his music were not passing fancies.

The string suite and the quartet, in conjunction with Flodin's unreserved recognition of their qualities, aroused, as we have said, great astonishment among the musical public of the Finnish capital, and through this Sibelius won admirers and friends in circles with which he had hitherto had no contact. One of these new friends was Robert Kajanus.

It may seem strange that he had not made the acquaintance of the well-known founder and director of the Helsinki Orchestra ere this. But it is comprehensible if one takes into consideration the keen competition existing between the two musical enterprises founded by Wegelius and Kajanus respectively in 1882: the Helsinki Musikförening, which was connected with the Academy of Music and arranged chamber music and solo concerts, and the Helsinki Orchestra Society (later the Philharmonic Society and from 1914 the Helsinki Municipal Orchestra), which sponsored the orchestra concerts.

This avalanche of musical activities all at once was a little too much for the city's essentially undeveloped musical public. Hence an active propaganda for their respective undertakings developed on both sides, leading to an implacable antagonism between the two competing interests. The partisans of each side had scarcely any personal intercourse, with the result that young Sibelius, as a pupil of the academy, never came into contact with the other active element in the musical life of the city.

Sibelius also thinks it very possible that this one-sidedness in his musical training, enforced by circumstances, may have been the reason why he turned his attention comparatively late to orchestral composition. The directors of the two opposing activities probably viewed the situation much more calmly than their supporters. Kajanus himself admitted that his relations with Wegelius "were good on the whole," which is shown by the fact that he was present at the academy concert, where he heard Sibelius' A minor quartet and made the composer's personal acquaintance.[2]

After hearing the quartet Kajanus is said to have remarked in his enthusiasm that now as far as he was concerned he might just as well give up composing. Wegelius' attitude, on the contrary, is said to have been far more reserved.

Before Sibelius left home to complete his studies in Germany, he wrote a chamber-music work in which he employed the expressive resources of music with far greater freedom than heretofore. This was a string quartet in B♭ Major characterized by Furuhjelm as "a more serious, mature, substantial, and more broadly treated counterpart of the violin sonata in F Major."

Sibelius' preoccupation with chamber-music style in all his first compositions was unquestionably advanta-

[2] Furuhjelm mentioned this in his work on Sibelius, and Kajanus told me personally several years before his death that the statement was correct. Ekman's assertion that the two met for the first time in Berlin is therefore erroneous. The Master himself no longer remembers exactly, but thinks it likely that they met at the performance in Helsinki.

geous. With limited instrumental resources, he acquired great facility in polyphonic writing and familiarity with larger cyclic forms. Flodin later described his impressions of these first chamber-music works (which are now very difficult of access, if at all extant) in a way that shows that they already bore all the hallmarks of the later works. "When I heard these strange quartets at the academy in which the polyphony was altogether orchestral and the form again and again manifested those individual characteristics that made the composer what he was, the thought struck me—how this young master will passionately convert to his own use all the wealth of orchestral color as soon as he has gained sufficient technical command of this form of expression! For me, these quartets were nothing more than sketches for later orchestral works."

Flodin's account of his first meeting with Sibelius and his description of this new and fascinating acquaintance probably shows better than any romantic account the impression made by the unique personality of the young music student. "There was something strangely winning about his slender figure. It was as if his upright, straightforward nature always wanted to meet one with open arms. Yet you were still not quite sure whether there was not some secret hokum back of it all. His conversation overflowed with paradoxical statements and ideas without one being able to say how much was serious and how much merely played on the surface, like bubbles of combinations and passing baroque whimsies generated in his nimble brain. His fair hair fell in disorderly strands on his forehead. His eyes had a veiled expression, but when his restless imagination began to work, they became more penetrating and took on a bluish shimmer. His ears were remarkable—large, well-shaped 'sound receivers,' the ears of a musician such as Beethoven must have had. . . . His conversation soon stalled like a hare in a thicket. But right on its heels came the musical ideas like hunting dogs. They seized and tore their prey and at the end turned their rapacious fangs on themselves. Before one knew it, Sibelius was juggling with colors and tones as though they were colored glass balls. He made the colors sound and the tones sparkle so that A Major was blue and C Major red, F Major green and D Major yellow, more or less; and everything in the world had its melodic label, every voice of nature its ready coined motif, every emotional impulse its primordial harmony, so that one could store the tones in little boxes and take them out again when they were needed. How could we ever imagine that a creative force was already dormant in this youth, that from these visions and fantasies that seemed to us so confused, so completely without any substantial foundation and connection, the framework of a new conception of the world was already in the making! I no longer remember how our meeting ended. But the portrait of Jean Sibelius had engraved itself on my consciousness from that moment on! I pricked up my ears whenever his name was mentioned, and when the friends of the academy were surprised by his first daring chamber-music works in which inspiration grappled wantonly with traditional forms and expressive resources—old leathern bottles that he wished to fill with his new wine—then his figure rose up before me as he appeared at our first meeting, plunging headlong into a sea of foaming ideas."

Equipped with a scholarship of the Nyland Student Corporation,[3] and with the object of obtaining a government grant, Sibelius went abroad for the first time in the autumn of 1889.

His first goal was Berlin, where on the advice of Wegelius he went to see Albert Becker, to whom the former had given him a letter of introduction, Becker at that time enjoying a great reputation as theorist and composer. Sibelius found him the very personification of musical conservatism. "I wrote fugues in strict style and other counterpoint for Becker [he said]. In musical matters the old man was extremely orthodox. 'Let it be *langweilig* so long as it's good style,' he used to say. *(Lieber langweilig, aber im Stil.)* With Becker I had to work hard and I wrote a lot of fugues, both instrumental and vocal, but all the time I couldn't help feeling that I was busying myself with things that belonged to the past; and now and then I lost patience."

In Berlin he entered into fruitful intercourse with young artists of every nationality, for the most part Scandinavians. His boyhood friend and countryman Adolf Paul, in his work *A Book about a Man,* gives a presumably highly romantic account of the lively meetings of the artists, in which Sibelius not only charmed the enthusiastic listeners with his clever and original ideas in word and pantomime but also with his arresting improvisations on the piano. Otherwise the young man was not overly impressed with Berlin. He found that despite its imposing outward development, it still corresponded in many ways to what he imagined it was like in the old Prussian days. Even the Germans of his acquaintance did not strike him as models from whom he could learn

3 The student corporations in Finland are organized according to the different provinces, each province having its own corporation or "Nation." Sibelius was a member of the "Nyland Corporation."

anything. He could not help feeling that, in many respects, the cultivated classes in Finland were considerably more advanced, and it contributed to his disappointment to find that here instead of new impulses in the field of music, he found only stagnation and sterility. "In the realm of music there was really nothing blanker than the transition to the nineties [he said] and the eighties were totally dominated by a decadence in art. (*Epigonentum.*) The conflict between the partisans of Brahms and Wagner engrossed all minds. The only young composer who enjoyed undisputed respect in Berlin was a certain August Bungert. His music was played a great deal and people seemed to look on him as a new Wagner! On the whole, the times were very pessimistic; and I was anything but a pessimist!" Although he took no active part in the Brahms-Wagner debate, Brahms's music was fundamentally more sympathetic to him; and still he could not work up any real enthusiasm for it. As for Wagner, in spite of the intensive Wagner propaganda that Wegelius fed his pupils in Helsinki—when he had relaxed his strictness a little—Sibelius' attitude towards him was very reserved even after he had heard *Meistersinger* and *Tannhäuser* in Berlin.

"The most important aspect of my stay in Berlin [he continued] was undoubtedly my being able to hear so much orchestral and ensemble music. At home I had to content myself with what I heard at the academy concerts and in private houses, but here one had the tremendously rich musical life of a great city and Germany's musical metropolis besides." In Berlin he became acquainted with most of the great musical masterpieces, from the perfect rendition of the last Beethoven quartets by the Joachim Quartet to such a sensational novelty as

Richard Strauss's *Don Juan*. And it was here also that he first heard Kajanus' Aino Symphony at the time of its performance by the Berlin Philharmonic Orchestra under the direction of the composer. Ekman's statement that Sibelius looked upon this work as the direct inspiration for his own symphonic poems based on the Kalevala (the corpus of Finnish mythology) was categorically denied by the Master in conversation with the present author. "That was something that matured in me quite by itself," he said; but he also added that it was something "that was in the air." At any rate he had grown up in a milieu far removed from the Kalevala[4] and during his youth, the Finnish folk *epos* was by no means so universally known as it was later. However, it should be pointed out that in all probability the Kullervo legend appealed to his imagination during his school days.

When he now says that the Kalevala, as a source of inspiration, was something "that was in the air," one can naturally take it for granted that Kajanus (like the painter Axel Gallen in his way) was one of the men who gave an impulse to the national idea. Be that as it may, the Master rejects the idea that the Aino Symphony played

[4] (Trans. note.) In the early part of the nineteenth century, Elias Lönrot, son of a village tailor, compiled an epic poem out of materials derived from Finnish folk poetry and mythology. The poem, written in the meter of *Hiawatha*, related the deeds and adventures of four heroes: Väinämöinen, the Orpheus of Finnish mythology and a powerful magician; Ilmarinen, his brother, a cunning artificer and smith; Lemminkäinen, a kind of northern Don Juan; Kullervo, a strange, somber figure. The other characters are Ilmatar, daughter of the air and mother of Väinämöinen; Aino, Väinämöinen's beloved; Louhi, mistress of the Northland and her daughter, the Maid of Pohjola who becomes the wife of Ilmarin. The poem contains fifty runes or cantos. Two English translations have been published, one by J. W. Crawford and one by W. F. Kirby, the latter obtainable in Everyman's Library (New York, E. P. Dutton & Co., Inc.).

any role in the conception of his own Kalevala work. Right from the beginning, he had planned his works from this circle of ideas along entirely different lines. As he says himself, he was extremely critical of Kajanus' work until the composer reworked it twenty-five years later, striking out a number of passages that had been strongly influenced by Wagner.

In addition to his very interesting coterie of acquaintances in Berlin and the inspiration derived from the city's musical activities behind the back of his strict mentor— who was anything but a proper guide at this stage of his career—Sibelius was busy working on a new chamber-music work—a piano quintet in G minor. External circumstances were certainly not conducive to the repose and concentration that he needed to carry out his project. Moreover he also lost his spiritual equilibrium at times, and during this winter underwent periods of deep depression despite his fundamentally optimistic disposition.

Technically, the quintet is about on a par with the works dating from his later Helsinki period. However, his treatment of several new ideas in figuration (the *tremolo,* for instance) heralded the awakening of a specifically orchestral and richly colored tonal fantasy. And as a matter of fact, after writing this work, he turned his attention more and more to the orchestra.

When summer came, the young student returned to Finland. During his comparatively short stay in his native land, he resumed his intercourse with the Järnefelt family, whom he had known before going abroad—an acquaintance that was to have an important bearing on his future. It is said that the house of Lieutenant General August Alexander Järnefelt was one of the few in Fin-

1889

1915 *(Photo Apollo)*

1935 *(Photo Pietinen)*

1953 *(Photo Levas)*

FOUR PORTRAITS OF JEAN SIBELIUS

land in which a convinced, strong Finnish national feeling was paired with a traditional and highly polished culture. Here Sibelius also came into contact with those young Finnish cultural aims that until then were almost unknown to a young composer brought up in a Swedish milieu. And it was in this circle that he eventually chose his wife. In the autumn of 1890 he became engaged to General Järnefelt's youngest daughter, Aino.

Later, in the autumn, he returned again to the continent, this time going to Vienna. Busoni had given him a letter of introduction to Brahms, but for some reason it failed entirely in its object. Brahms obstinately refused to receive him. Sibelius finally made the acquaintance of the idolized master in a Vienna café, although, as he says, the meeting made no deep impression on him.

The Brahms-Wagner feud was, if possible, even more passionate in Vienna than in Berlin. But that did not prevent Hans Richter (the famous Wagner conductor to whom Wegelius had also given him a letter of introduction) from recommending to him a teacher of orchestration from the enemy camp, namely, Robert Fuchs, one of the leading men of the Brahms front. Along with his studies under Fuchs's conscientious guidance, Sibelius also enjoyed on several occasions the advice of Carl Goldmark, whose fame as a composer at that time was almost equal to that of Brahms and Bruckner.

It has been said that a trace of orchestral fantasy can be found from time to time in Sibelius' chamber music of this period. On the other hand one finds that in his earliest orchestral works the polyphonic treatment of the thematic material, which is a natural expressive medium for a wealth of ideas in the transparent texture of chamber music, does not let the orchestral tone stand out clearly enough in relief *(plastik)* but makes the work seem a little overloaded. "My orchestral style [he admitted] was at this time still governed entirely by chamber-music style, from which it was very difficult to free myself. It was only after I had returned to Finland towards the end of the nineties that I was able to develop a real orchestral style."

It can be taken for granted that Sibelius' studies with Fuchs broadened his technical knowledge of orchestration in many ways and also gradually increased his assurance in the treatment of the orchestra. "But neither my studies with Fuchs nor those with Goldmark were of much importance for my inner development [he continued]. And while I was in process of making a routined orchestrator of myself, I couldn't resist paying homage once more to the great love of my youth—chamber music. I wrote a piano quartet in C Major with which my teachers had nothing to do."

This quartet, his last chamber-music work before he abandoned this genre for orchestral music for two decades, is never mentioned in earlier works on his life and career, although other youthful compositions have been copiously cited and analyzed by Furuhjelm, among others. Early in the nineteen thirties I came across the manuscript of the quartet in a private house and made a copy of it. There is every reason to say that it is in a key scheme of C minor since one gains the impression that this key dominates the work, which consists of an introduction in C Major and a theme with variations in C minor. The *adagio* introduction, which is related to the theme introduced immediately afterwards, is almost orchestral in conception, with characteristic *tremolo* passages in the strings (two violins and one cello) and a highly figured, rumbustious piano part. The theme itself is simple and in popular national style *(folkligt)*:

EXAMPLE 1

One would almost be tempted to say it was marked with a typically Finnish melancholy if the trochaic rhythm were not anything but Finnish. The variations of the grateful theme are very diverse and colorful and reveal, as well, individual traits that seem characteristic of the young composer's orchestral fantasy, which developed so richly during the ensuing decade.

Sibelius' first essay in writing for the orchestra was an overture, which Goldmark (according to the Master) literally "tore to pieces." Soon after this he wrote another —an overture in E Major—which found greater favor in his teacher's eyes. He sent this overture and another orchestral work *(A Ballet Scene)* to Helsinki where they were performed at Kajanus' orchestral concerts in the spring of 1891.

It is not so easy to get a clear idea of Sibelius' youthful works since the Master is no longer willing to make them available to the public. We are therefore dependent on the statements of others. "Like all compositions of this highly gifted composer [wrote Flodin after the first performance], this was no ordinary overture either as regards form or content. Sibelius is now definitely going his own way; whether he does so consciously is an open question. However, it is true on the whole that, undeterred by traditional rules, he hearkens solely to the inspirations of his own genius, since this genius is so incontestably original and individualistic. One needs only to listen once to this effervescent overture, brimming over with ideas!" Furuhjelm spoke of the overture as being "a little overweighted by its imposing polyphony." Otherwise he considered it an effective opening number with "its mixture of solemnity and elegiac lyricism, and several quite fantastic metamorphoses relieving one another." The ballet music, which in texture was more orchestral and transparent, he characterized as "a more perfect and homogeneous creation as regards form." Here Sibelius was "quite worldly minded," in one instance "quite unequivocally cosmopolitan." The composition therefore represents "something quite unique in his creative work." It is a very romantic affair that "vividly suggests a nocturnal intermezzo raised to a fantastic plane."

The winter in the city on the Danube was, it seems, far more productive than the previous one in Berlin. Besides the quartet and the first orchestral works, he wrote several songs to texts by Runeberg, drafted the first sketches of a Kullervo symphony and began an octet for strings, flute and clarinet, which contained the germ of the later *En Saga*.

He liked Vienna much better than the German capital. For his leisure hours he found some real friends in a coterie of young musicians and artists whom he saw daily and through whom he joined an anti-Wagnerian student orchestra. At that time Vienna was still the old Vienna despite the Wagner-Brahms feud. Johann Strauss, Jr. was still alive, and Sibelius had an opportunity from time to time of hearing him conduct his waltzes. His love for them dates from these days, and he has been faithful to them all his life. The power of musical tradition was then unbroken, and the air was laden with memories and verbal traditions dating not only from the days of Schubert and Beethoven but even from the time of Mozart. Here the young artist lived and composed in a very stimulating environment, and even though he was not spared periods of doubt and depression, they still did not afflict him as often as in the previous winter in Berlin. He now perceived more clearly than before the goals for which he had to strive. He had more self-assurance, was confident of his mission, and did not let himself be led astray in spite of his teachers' comparative lack of understanding for the individualistic style that he now began to realize was his strong point.

His return to Finland in the summer of 1891 marked the end of his real student years. In his book, *The Ro-*

mance of My Parents, Arvid Järnefelt described his impressions of the young Sibelius and sketched a portrait of his sister's fiancé that furnishes a lifelike picture of the strangely sensitive and impulsive nature of the young genius. "At that time Sibelius was really so fresh and full of life, so carried away with the pulsating realities of life, and his enthusiasm was so generally contagious that he could not help but enchant all those who came into contact with him. He was a young man who knew how to enjoy everything—a good cigar, a conversation, jolly company, the life of nature. When one saw him out in the country, were it only a meadow, one was aware that even here he was living his own full, individual life. The twittering of a bird, and he was immediately all ears; the call of a young shepherdess, and the melody passed for all time into his soul. He was exceedingly receptive and everything born of the moment, every sound that caught his ear, everything within his range of vision, was transmuted into "Sibelius." He lived every minute so intensively that he sometimes reminded one of an animal, of a fish springing through the rapids, of a young hunting dog panting for breath while starting the game, or of a bird, which even when quiet on its perch, moves its head in order to catch the slightest rustle and note everything that life round it has to communicate to it."

Inspirations from the Kalevala

*W*hen Sibelius stepped out before a wider public, nationalism in music was already the order of the
day in Europe. The Slavs had made their way; Tchaikovsky was taken—rightly or wrongly—as the typical Russian; Liszt had written his Hungarian Rhapsodies and
inspired others in Italy, Spain, Norway, Sweden, and
Finland to do the same. With the newly awakened interest in ethnography as point of departure, musical impressions of nature and the life of the people were composed on every hand. The whole tendency, which in the
main utilized the melodic treasures of folk music, was a
typical offshoot of the late romanticism of this century.

The works composed within the circle of the Musical
Society, founded in Turku in 1790, and the Academy of
Music, established and developed in old Helsinki in the
nineteenth century by Fredrik Pacius, though unpre-
tentious from an international standpoint, were of far-
reaching national importance. With Karl Collan, Axel
Gabriel Ingelius, Filip von Schantz, and Robert Kajanus
as leading figures, Finland also began to take an interest
in music reflecting national feelings and racial idiom,
which was so vigorously nurtured in the romantic age
and whose rich ethnographic material had hitherto not
been utilized artistically.

The presumably first attempt to write specifically "national" music associated with Finnish mythology is the Kullervo Overture, preserved among von Schantz' effects. (He died the year of Sibelius' birth.) The attempts of Collan, Ingelius, and von Schantz to create a national Finnish music took place in the first epoch of the national awakening, under the influence of the general enthusiasm. And even though their effects, either from the national or the aesthetic viewpoint, were not overly important, the idea was by no means dead. About twenty-five years later it was taken up again by Kajanus, whose national importance as a composer is based on the fact that he called attention to the musical possibilities of the Kalevala myths (Kullervo Funeral March, Aino Symphony) and to the thematic suitability of Finnish folk music for art music (Finnish Rhapsodies, etc.). That he was influenced by his teacher Johan Svendsen and used highly Germanic, and at times even Wagnerian, expressive resources, diminishes in no way his importance as the forerunner of a national Finnish music.

Sibelius' first creative work was also influenced by the national awakening. But with a decisive difference, as compared with his forerunners. In so far as he was inspired by the zeal of the national movement to collect and transform ethnographic material, it—in his case—was more on a literary-mythological than a musical-ethnographical plane. This does not mean that in his Kalevala tone poem he is "literary" in the sense of programmatic details, but that he created and developed his peculiar mythological-romantic style under the influence of this epic itself and never felt tempted to employ folk-song motifs at the expense of his own invention. Among the external factors that had great bearing on his development, one can perhaps perceive certain slight traces of the stylistic features of Finnish folk music in his work; but where this is the case, the influence is only indirect and of secondary importance. However, where his Kalevala music breathes a distinctly individual quality, something that it is difficult to characterize, something that one can call specifically Finnish, we can venture to assume that with the instinct of genius he captured and absorbed something of the atmosphere of Finnish folk music, and that at times his art borrowed its color and its musical idiom from this. A. O. Väisänen (very likely the greatest authority on Finnish runic melodies) in a thorough examination of Sibelius' works succeeded in identifying only a couple of isolated folk-music motif germs. But these more solid particles from the ethnographic atmosphere have been filtered to such insignificance through his unconscious and unintentional act of conception that they have had no influence on his style, his form, or his thematic treatment, if, taking it all round, it is a question of something other than a mere accidental resemblance between these motif fragments, i.e., wholly independent motifs stemming only from the same "local" and psychological premises—we can add with reservation.

Sibelius' first youthful works show no traces of any Finnish nationalistic interests. At that time his music was inspired with a purely Scandinavian spirit and he lived and created under the influence of Finnish-Swedish and Scandinavian literature. From the very beginning his instrumental works were very individual in style and the vocal works were based almost exclusively on Swedish texts.

However, the increased study of, and absorption in, the mythological world of the Kalevala was still of funda-

mental importance, and he became conscious of the hitherto undreamt-of possibilities slumbering in the Finnish
national epic, which cried out for a great artistic realization—a predestined task for a person of his temperament.

His immediate environment in the Finland of the
nineties conduced in every way to stimulate his sympathy
for Finnish nationalistic aspirations. At that time the
country was passing through a period of extraordinary
political activity. The decrees promulgated by the Russian authorities in 1890, which represented the first serious menace[1] to Finland's laws and rights, aroused a
patriotic enthusiasm that found the best possible soil in
the already awakened nationalistic movement. Through
his future brothers-in-law, Arvid, Eero, and Armas Järnefelt (one of whom was a poet, another a painter, and the
third a musician) Sibelius was initiated into the circle
associated with the newspaper "Päivälehti"—a center of
activity whose object was to awaken the patriotism of
the Finnish people. All hopes were then set on a heightened cultural activity; and national art (which had just
begun to develop) and a high educational level were
looked upon as the country's surest moral bulwark.

In this coterie of authors and other artists, Sibelius
was one of the representatives of music. The dissimilarity
in the professional training and interests united these
enthusiastic "banner bearers of civilization" more than
it divided them. Here Sibelius met among others the
painter Axel Gallen, to whom he was bound from then
on by ties of an intimate and profitable friendship.
Among the other friends he made in Helsinki during

[1] In 1890 the Imperial Russian authorities issued the so-called
"Postal Manifest," the purpose of which was the Russification of the
Finnish postal and monetary systems by placing them under the cogni-
zance of the corresponding Russian departments.

these animated and fruitful years, which were brimming over with new ideas in every realm of art, were the writers Juhani Aho, Karl August Tavastjerna, Adolf Paul, and Mikael Lybeck. But there were still many others who with their poetry and writings nourished Sibelius' creative imagination in the field of vocal lyrics and incidental music for the stage.

When he then began to contribute his own share of original creative works, it was amid a company of active talents, and the first goal that he set himself was to finish the great Kullervo work, the preliminary sketches of which he had already made in Vienna. An especially favorable spur to creation during this period was the community of ideas and intimate association with Gallen, who was working at that time on his famous *Aino* triptych.

In the spring of 1892 he gave the finishing touches to the proud creation that Furuhjelm called "the rebellious prologue to the achievements of his manhood," namely, the Kullervo Symphony. This work, which was truly revolutionary at that time, is a great symphonic poem—it has been called a symphony—in five movements for large orchestra, soloists, and chorus. The first movement, which forms the introduction and sounds the keynote of the work, gives musical expression to numerous moods of mythical northern wastes within a broad symphonic framework, but it also contains a number of allusions to the real drama and "foreshadows several phrases of the tragedy."

In the second movement *(Kullervo's Youth)*, which is somber in color throughout, there are no dramatic moments in an outward sense. The movement is to be understood rather as expressive of the gloomy brooding attitude of the hero, broken at intervals by elegiac tone pictures of the idyllic solitudes. In the third movement *(Kullervo and his Sister)* the hero sets forth in youthful spirits with jingling sleigh bells and at headlong speed on fateful adventures that culminate in a drama of incest.[2]

This movement is rich in highly effective contrasts: a wild climax, lyrical moods of the dawning day, an idyllic picture of nature, and the simple tale of the sister. Then, in contrast, the epilogue: Kullervo's pathetic lament when he learns the identity of the girl whose honor he has besmirched. The fourth movement *(Kullervo Goes Forth to Battle)* gives this work its heroic cast. Sibelius draws his picture of the red-blooded hero of antiquity with a blend of realism and singular archaism. In the fifth movement *(The Death of Kullervo)* the spiritual conflicts come to a head with the return of the fate motif from the first movement, which here pictures the inner struggles of the hero. The entire mood is somber and

2 (Trans. note.) The adventures of Kullervo are told in Cantos XXI and XXXVI of the Kalevala. Kullervo, on his way homeward in his sleigh, pays court in vain to two maidens, and finally wins a third by gifts and cajolery, only to discover after it was too late that she was his sister from whom he had been parted since infancy. The maiden, stricken by remorse, throws herself into a neighboring torrent and is drowned. Kullervo tries in vain to find oblivion in various warlike activities. Then finally, with his faithful dog at his side, takes his way through the forest until he comes to the spot where the fatal meeting with his sister had taken place, and there, drawing his sword,

> On the ground the haft set firmly,
> On the heath the hilt pressed tightly,
> Turned the point against his bosom,
> And upon the point he threw him,
> Thus he found the death he sought for,
> Cast himself into destruction.
> Even so the young man perished,
> Thus died Kullervo the hero,
> Thus the hero's life was ended,
> Perished thus the hapless hero.

oppressive, and Kullervo's fate finally ends in a lament rising to a powerful climax with strident dissonances. In the epilogue the tragic main motif of the introduction returns again, this time in splendid orchestration. And the drama is over.

Kullervo is, for its time, an extraordinarily daring and powerful work. In its "contempt for the conventional, for *bon ton,* and the taste of the public, it can measure swords with the most audacious works written by European masters during the nineteenth century [wrote Furuhjelm]. It is the most extreme of Sibelius' works in a certain direction, in the same way, for example, as the Fourth Symphony in another direction. It is a work of gigantic but fascinating proportions and set against the European musical background at the time of its creation, it must be viewed as epoch-making. It is not the most harmonious of Sibelius' mythological works. There are many rough, unpolished passages in it. But it is the most imposing and interesting of its type."

We may add that *Kullervo* has never kindled any interest abroad because it has never been performed outside the boundaries of Sibelius' native land. But it is still interesting to see how this work was received by the fairly inexperienced and innocent Helsinki public of the nineties. As a matter of fact, all eyewitnesses agree that it aroused far greater enthusiasm than any native work heretofore. A hall packed to the doors and the stormiest ovations. In previous performances of works by the young genius, a good bit of astonishment and skepticism was mingled with the enthusiasm. But now everyone was so dumbfounded, impressed, and fascinated at the same time that they succumbed to it without giving the matter much thought. They applauded and ad-

mired it even though they could not quite grasp it. Some
of the enthusiasm can perhaps be laid to the national
awakening and the patriotism generated by other causes.

The critics were clever enough—this time, at least—
to follow the example of the public. Some of them made
almost touching efforts to produce the impression that
they understood what it was all about, and others appeared to look upon it as a gripping and ingenious curios-
ity despite its abstruseness; but at all events none dared
run the risk of adverse criticism. Even though there was
some doubt regarding his trends and intentions. Sibelius'
talent was beyond all discussion. In his own country he
had carried the day once and for all.

Still even the most intelligent commentators were
guilty of a fatal error, which was repeated for decades all
the world over, in evaluating Sibelius' work. It was admitted that the composition, the psychological config-
urations, and the technical treatment were quintessen-
tial Sibelius, but it was generally assumed that he had
derived his thematic material from folk music. "He
found the tone he sought in the peculiar idiom of the
Runic singers, in the rhythms of the folk dances, in the
clang of the shepherd's horn." wrote Flodin, the only
critic, by the way, who qualified his praise with a number
of reservations.

Sibelius' own statement should be set over against
this. "As a musician and as the composer of *Kullervo* I
had particular interest in visiting the Karelian country-
side. There I could still hear the old runes, after having
sunk myself so intensively in the world whose moods,
fate, and people they describe. The idiom that I employed in *Kullervo* is such a perfect and true expression
of the Finnish scenery and the Finnish soul that many

said that I must have made direct use of folk melodies, especially the cadences and intonation of the old Runic singers. But I could not have achieved the genuinely Finnish idiom in *Kullervo,* as was assumed, for the very simple reason that when I wrote the work, I was still ignorant of my supposed models. First I composed *Kullervo* and then I went to Karelia to hear, for the first time in my life, the Kalevala runes from the lips of the people."

Kullervo is Sibelius' most noteworthy composition dating from the early nineties and his first work in the mythological-romantic genre. It thus represents a fundamental introduction, which has been followed by a series of important symphonic poems that showed how deeply he had penetrated into the mythical period of the Kalevala. And he simplifies, varies, and renews his style without cessation.

On June 10, 1892, Sibelius married Aino Järnefelt, a highly cultivated and refined personality who is still her husband's faithful companion. From the first decades of a marriage blessed with many children up to the later years with their increasing burden of international renown, she has been able to create, and maintain, in their home—with a firm yet gentle hand—the homish, tranquil atmosphere that is an indispensable prerequisite to the Master's creative work. The young couple spent their honeymoon in Karelia, where Sibelius made his first acquaintance with the Finnish runic melodies.

From the autumn of 1892, we find him permanently engaged as teacher of composition at the Academy of Music in Helsinki and as second violin in the school's string quartet. He likewise taught composition in the orchestral school of the Philharmonic Society, a position that Robert Kajanus (a more enthusiastic Sibelius admirer than ever after he had heard *Kullervo*) had created for him in order to help him out financially.

"And that was not the only evidence of Kajanus' energetic interest in me," confessed Sibelius gratefully. "It was of immense importance to me to have him place his orchestra so completely at the service of my art—partly by placing it at my disposal whenever I wanted to try out the effects of certain tonal combinations, or wished to hear how my scores really sounded. Kajanus' encouraging attitude furthered, to a very great degree, my development as an orchestral composer during the last decade of the nineteenth century, and I owe him a debt of gratitude for everything he did for me not only in my youth but also in later years; for the truly understanding champions of my art were none too numerous."

Along with his teaching duties, which were quite onerous (he had sometimes as many as thirty teaching hours a week), he was busy completing some compositions that he had begun in the summer, among them a larger work for orchestra, the genesis of which is usually associated with an anecdote that Sibelius himself, however, characterizes as apocryphal. After the successful *Kullervo* concert, Kajanus asked him to write an orchestral work in "somewhat popular style" that "would not place too high demands on the public." "But nothing came of it," said Sibelius. "Instead I completed the orchestral work I had already started and to which I gave the name *En Saga*. This tone poem (which takes eighteen minutes to perform) was by no means the result of Kajanus' request to write 'a popular *Da capo* piece'! I did not comply with his request." *En Saga* is therefore designedly a highly serious symphonic poem, or as Sigurd Frosterus characterized it more than forty years later, "a brilliant orchestral adventure without programmatic basis, a haughty, lordly poem of chivalry with pungent rhythms and motifs in phrases oscillating between northern melancholy and southern passion. Sparkling fireworks up and down the hot and cold tones of the spectrum, wherein it amused Sibelius to paint freely just as he pleased."

En Saga was performed for the first time in February, 1893, in Helsinki and in 1901 was thoroughly revised. Then it was published. The original score is still extant and a comparative analysis of the two versions is both interesting and instructive, especially for the initiated musician. The comparison shows very clearly how Sibelius developed from a genial and ruthlessly independent artist to a master with a sovereign command of all his expressive resources. Perhaps the first version shows greater originality, but as a composition and a masterpiece of technique, the second version is on a higher level. And paradoxical as this may sound, the ruthless tonal homogeneity (or stubbornness) of the second version (as exemplified in the one-hundred-bar pedal point, for instance, and the disinclination to change the key) seems, in its sovereign disdain of any fear of monotony, not only more daring, but more thrilling in effect than the greater modulatory richness of the first version. The transitions also give the impression of more organically developed units, and the orchestration in the final version is throughout more colorful and richly differentiated.

It is curious to see how differently the various critics interpret the psychological background of *En Saga*. For Olin Downes, the American Sibelius enthusiast, the music conjures up the picture of a land on the extreme northern boundary of European civilization where the pagan gods still hold sway and where trolls and mermaids are as familiar as tame house pets. He calls the second theme of the viola "a barbaric dance theme," and when in the concluding portion he seems to hear "a dance with knives drawn," he "avows a carnal desire to discard the soft fat ways of life, to set out in oilskins, or something, for somewhere, to discover at least a desperate polar bear bent on conflict"! Sibelius' first true champion in the Anglo-Saxon world, Rosa Newmarch, proceeds from the theory that this music surely refers to the narration of some old tale in which the heroic and touching elements are cleverly combined. And a German critic, Ernst Tansberger, asserts *ex cathedra* that the "tone poem is based on a legend from Finland's mythical past." Erik Furuhjelm comes obviously nearer the truth when—without indulging in literary interpretations—he speaks of the "fantasy and legendary mysticism of *En Saga*" and of its "strange images and superhuman impressions." On the other hand one must emphatically reject his claim that this symphonic poem is rhapsodic in effect and contains no "real main theme," in fact, not "even a leading idea of any kind." An analysis of the composition shows the direct contrary.

The most natural way to grasp this composition, but one that proves strangely difficult for so many foreigners, is to take it simply as a legend *without* any literary or programmatic basis, as one that Sibelius *himself* invented and that he, even had he wished, could not perhaps narrate with words—to take it purely as a fantastic legend that only the iridescent and mobile language of music is capable of expressing. As Frosterus said, it amused Sibelius "to paint freely just as he pleased." "One follows the colorful episodes with breathless attention. It is a distinct relief to meet the romantic hero-type himself, and not some labeled representative of the genre." Diktonius also (without presupposing any concrete dramatic action) speaks very pertinently of a "folk epic in romantic dress. What it narrates is as simple as a folksong, dour as the lonely wastes, and brilliant as the princess and half the kingdom."

During this period a series of evening meetings took place of which Gallen caught a characteristic moment in the realistic-symbolic painting *The Symposium,* which at that time was so fiercely attacked by the contemporary moralists. At these certainly not unfruitful meetings, with their mutual interchange of ideas over a glass of wine, the trio Sibelius, Gallen, and Kajanus formed the solid core round which clustered other like-minded artists and sometimes also a couple of representatives of the profane mob. "We allowed our imagination to soar and our thoughts to play [said Sibelius]. The waves rolled very high. Life passed in review. We discussed the most diverse questions but always in an optimistic and revolutionary spirit. The way was to be cleared for new ideas in all fields. The Symposium evenings were a great stimulus to me at a time when otherwise I should have stood more or less alone. The opportunity of exchanging ideas with kindred souls, animated by the same spirit and the same objectives, had an extremely stimulating effect on me. It strengthened my resolutions and gave me confidence."

In the nineties Helsinki was a small town, but it was an example to many a larger place in its appreciation of art and artists. As already mentioned, a high cultural level was considered the country's surest defense against the threat from the east, and one realized what one owed to the standard-bearers of this culture. Everyone knew about the Symposium meetings and comments were usually good natured. Gossip was rife and fantastic rumors were current regarding the physical endurance of the members.

It was quite natural for such a generous and condescending person as Sibelius, to accept commissions for more or less occasional compositions. And one can call it our good fortune that this was so, for a large part of this commissioned music (after being worked over—a labor he usually reserved for later) is among the most important that he wrote, such, for instance, as the *Karelia Suite* and the two suites *Historic Scenes* and *Finlandia*.

Among the external stimuli for Sibelius' art, myth and fable were for long the most fructifying. However, from the moment the Viborg Student Corporation requested him to write the musical accompaniment for a series of tableaux depicting incidents in Karelia's ancient history (for an evening performance in aid of national education in eastern Finland), history also became an inspirational force in his creative work. In the original version the music was intended only to form a musical background for the historical tableaux. Not until it was revised as an independent concert suite did this remarkable composition receive its just due. When it was first performed, the *Karelia Suite* comprised eight numbers, but soon thereafter the composer subjected it to a stricter revision, reducing it to an overture and a suite of three movements.

The *Karelia* music has very little in common with what one usually calls descriptive program music, which as far as the nature of the material and the motive for its composition are concerned, might well have been the case. And still it has a very specific atmospheric background. We can say with Furuhjelm that on one hand it is full of chivalrous, warlike elements, and that on the other hand it reflects the popular and rustic. In the overture these contrasting psychological elements combine to give a general picture of the period and milieu.

In the winter of 1893–94, Sibelius was extraordinarily productive. He composed numerous songs and piano pieces, and from the spring of this year dates the beautiful hymn to northern nature entitled *Vårsång (Spring Song)*, whose mixture of springtide joy and melancholy yearning is perhaps more correctly rendered by the French subtitle *La tristesse du printemps*. It is necessary to point out, however, that this latter title does not derive from Sibelius himself. It is an invention of the publishers and is misleading, in the composer's opinion. The English Sibelius connoisseur Cecil Gray also rejects it. He concedes at most "a strain of wistful and elegiac melancholy in the middle minor section" but otherwise "the mood is tranquil and serene throughout." "An elegiac mood of the freshest expectation [reads Frosterus' lovely description of the work] from a widening firmament and rapidly receding horizon sounds shyly and warily from the demurest themes Sibelius ever invented. The northern soil from which his music has sprung has never brought forth a purer, lovelier flower than this dewsprent hymn to the promises of life looming in the future."

During a summer sojourn in Kuopio in 1893, Sibelius in his conversations with the writer J. H. Erkko got the idea of writing an opera based on a Kalevala motif, which was to be called *Weneen luominen (Creation of the Boat)*. With Erkko as literary adviser, Sibelius himself undertook to write the libretto, which he completed, together with a prologue, during the summer. This opera, however, was never finished. It was considered much "too lyrical," but the composer's work was not entirely wasted, since the renewed absorption in the world of the Kalevala gave him the idea for a great Lemminkäinen suite for orchestra, one number of which was already written, that is, *The Swan of Tuonela*. At the turn of the year 1895–96 the tetralogy was completed and the first performance of the four orchestral legends— *Lemminkäinen and the Maidens, Lemminkäinen in Tuonela, The Swan of Tuonela,* and *The Return of Lemminkäinen*—took place on April 13, 1896. Soon after this he revised the cycle and the new version was performed at two concerts of new music in November, 1897. *The Swan of Tuonela* and *The Return of Lemminkäinen* were revised a second time in 1900 and were then published. The other two scores were lost for thirty years but came to light again at the beginning of the thirties. The Master had already corrected the last proofs and had just despatched them to Breitkopf & Härtel in Leipzig when World War II broke out, so that for a time their fate was uncertain, but they have since been published and are also now available in miniature scores.

The title of the first symphonic poem presents a problem to anyone who desires to link the inspirational source with a definite episode of the Kalevala. There are actually two titles. In the performance in the nineties it bore the title *Lemminkäinen and the Maidens on the Island,* but after the score was found it has always been known as *Lemminkäinen and the Saari (island) Maidens.* The first title apparently has reference to the verses in the twenty-ninth canto of the Kalevala which picture the gallant adventures of the hero on a lonely island, that is, his journey

> Forward to the nameless island,
> And the nameless promontory.   (29: 41–42)

The second title refers to the island (Saari) mentioned in the eleventh canto, wherein the course of events is similar and yet differs in one important point, namely, the wild doings of the hero with a group of beautiful maidens, which is here not an end in itself (as in the twenty-ninth canto) but merely the prelude to his effort to win the hand of the arrogant Kyllikki—an object that he ultimately achieves by carrying her off by force. Hence the dramatic development in the last section of the tone poem seems to me to refer to the second episode with the rape of the beautiful Kyllikki, although when I questioned the Master regarding this, he declined to say whether or not this was his intention. He only went so far as to state that it is correct to view the island episode as the background of the work, adding that he merely wished to portray the wanton life of the hero and not any specific action in detail. As such, it is a fascinating orchestral work depicting the lively pranks and capers of a carefree young lover, with a touch of glowing passion and youthful bravado.

In the nineties *The Swan of Tuonela* formed Part II

of the suite, but after finding the long-lost scores, Sibelius wished to reverse the order of Parts II and III. This arrangement now seems more natural and logical from the standpoint of musical form and the Kalevala epic as well. The purpose of the tone picture of the realm of the black river of death[3] (which is quite independent in itself) is, with respect to the suite as a whole, to picture the scene of the mournful drama that took place when Lemminkäinen

> Went and took his twanging crossbow,
> Went away to seek the long neck,
> Forth to Tuoni's murky river. (14: 385–387)

The work is scored for an orchestra in which all the bright-toned instruments are excluded from the scheme: a *cor anglais* solo for the mournful song of the swan, one oboe, one bass clarinet, bassoons, horns, trombones, harp, kettledrums, bass drum, and muted strings divided into an immense number of parts. Frosterus, in a single sentence, has picturesquely captured the strange atmosphere of this celebrated work. "The somber melodic coils of the swan's siren call float metallically over the river while the bewitching light of the underworld throws colored sparks into the glittering whirlpool and the waters, gliding away from the precipitous banks of the Realm of the Dead spread gloom and icy terror over all."

The third number of the suite after the Master's rearrangement *(Lemminkäinen in Tuonela)* refers to the events narrated in the fourteenth and fifteenth cantos of

---

[3] The inscription on the score reads: "Tuonela, the land of death, the hell of Finnish mythology, is surrounded by a large river with black waters and a rapid current on which the Swan of Tuonela floats majestically, singing."

the Kalevala. In order to win the Daughter of the North, the hero must perform three heroic deeds. Two of these he has already accomplished. Only the third remains.

> I will only give my daughter
> Give the youthful bride you seek for,
> If the river swan you shoot me,
> Shoot the great bird on the river.
> There on Tuoni's murky river,
> In the sacred river's whirlpool,
> Only at a single trial,
> Using but a single arrow.   (14:375–82)

On the banks of the river the hero falls a victim to the treacherous attack of a cowherd from Pohjola.[4]

> Then the blood-stained son of Tuoni,
> Drew his sword and smote the hero,
> With his gleaming blade he slew him,
> While it shed a stream of flashes,
> And he hewed him in five fragments,
> Then in Tuonela's stream cast them. (14:445–51)

Lemminkäinen's mother, who is waiting at home, notices that blood is trickling from her son's comb which reveals to her that death has overtaken him, so she sets forth to seek him. After many trials and wanderings she finds his trail and manages to persuade the clever smith Ilmarinen to forge her a gigantic rake with which she rakes the entire river, fishes out the different fragments of Lemminkäinen's body, joins them together, and succeeds in restoring him to life by charms and magic balsams.

The mournful main *Tuonela* theme rises from the cellos and double basses like a vision from the dark eddy-

---

4 Pohjola, the Northern Land.

ing waters of the River of the Dead until after an "anguish-filled" *(ångestfullt) stringendo,* it stalls in an *ostinato* accompanying figure. Against this background the woodwinds then introduce the description of the macabre events.

A strange thematic relationship existing between a germ motif right at the beginning

EXAMPLE 2

and the germ of the main subject

EXAMPLE 3

in the last tone poem of the cycle, *The Return of Lemminkäinen,* is worthy of attention. The similarity and the predominant role of the motif in the two tone poems impelled me to ask the Master if it was correct to consider this motif a sort of leitmotif personifying the hero. To this he replied very definitely: "Even though it is impossible to deny the resemblance, this was neither intentional nor conscious. The leitmotif technique has always been foreign to my mode of thought; there is something too calculatingly purposive about it."

This emphatic statement seems to me to be of fundamental importance and represents an authoritative as well as scathing rejection of those recent programmatic interpretations of Sibelius' symphonies based on a minute analysis of the motifs. The printed score of the fourth and last of the tone poems of the suite *(The Return of Lemminkäinen)* contains an explanatory note in German and French in which the protagonist of the work is characterized as a hero, as the Achilles of Finnish mythology, whose intrepidity and beauty made him the favorite of women. Weary of his military adventures he decides to return home.

> Then the lively Lemminkäinen
> From his cares constructed horses,
> Coursers black composed from trouble,
> Reins from evil days he fashioned,
> Saddles from his secret sorrows,
> Then his horse's back he mounted,
> On his white-front courser mounted,
> And he rode upon his journey.   (30:481–89)

After many adventures he reaches his own country at last, rejoicing at the sight of the familiar scenes with all their childhood memories.

At the beginning the thematic material of the symphonic poem seems to consist only of tiny scraps and fragments that are tossed about from one group of instruments to another. But they are gradually welded together into little organic themes, which with meager instrumental resources, are employed to create a feeling of tension and energy that never slackens for a moment and are finally unleashed in the brilliant, triumphant triad passages of the *stretto* to produce a towering orchestral climax.

This working with small motif fragments, which is typical of Sibelius' orchestral style, is also found in other compositions of the cycle. It is only more pronounced in the last symphonic poem. Here the gradual development of the motif fragments to a gay, bold main subject passes through four different developmental stages in the course of a couple of hundred bars (which also employ still other motifs) the last stage of which (d) represents the fully developed main theme.

EXAMPLE 4

In stage (b) a bassoon voice is added to the fragment, which rounds it off in a very clear, decisive manner.

EXAMPLE 5

But at the repetition, which follows immediately, this bassoon voice assumes the character of an entirely new motif

EXAMPLE 6

which also plays an important thematic role in the continuation.

With this reference to one of the many peculiarities

of the thematic technique of the *Lemminkäinen Suite,* I
have only wished to call attention to the original—one
might say the ruthlessly personal—manner of Sibelius'
earliest orchestral style, not only as regards the shimmering nuances but also the structure. In addition one can
also detect in it a presage of the structural method characteristic of his later symphonic style, which will be discussed later in connection with the Sixth Symphony.

Viewed in relation to the whole, *The Return of
Lemminkäinen* represents a spirited, impetuously on-
rushing, yet fundamentally clear and idyllic finale for a
fantastically rich work, which touches strings of emotions and moods that span the extreme poles of human
existence: life raised to its nth power, and death to the
uttermost limit.

No wonder this work aroused misgivings among the
contemporary critics. At that time one was far more in-
clined "to enjoy" more or less idyllically beautiful music.
Faced with something entirely new, with an art that demanded of the listener the utmost in emotional response
and sailed blissfully over the paltriness of the hedonistic
ideal of beauty, the public quite understandably did not
know what to make of it. Even Flodin, still the most far-
sighted and intelligent writer on music in Finland at that
time, could not give his approval to music of this sort.
Although he stated emphatically that he was no Hanslick, who "with a hypocritical glance at the classic and
romantic masters coldly and systematically pronounced
an anathema against all new art from which an individuality emerges that creates new tones and new forms," he
wrote of the *Lemminkäinen Suite* among other things:
"This kind of music is downright pathological and leaves
such a mixed, painful, and in the last analysis, indefinable

impression that it has very little in common with that aesthetic enjoyment that all beautiful art—and music above all—should arouse." Although written by an enthusiastic and orthodox Wagnerian, the sentence, as paradoxical as it may seem, might well have been written by a Hanslick—about Wagner, for example.

III

At the Turn of the Century

In the summer of 1894, we find Sibelius on one of the foreign tours that he made practically every year during his forties. His goal this time was Italy, where the scenery, the historical background, and the life of the people made a deep impression on him. At the urgent request of his brother-in-law, the enthusiastic Wagnerian, Armas Järnefelt, he joined the latter in Bayreuth on his way home, but he could work up no more enthusiasm for Wagner now than before. In fact the whole atmosphere of Bayreuth with its exaggerated reverence seems rather to have intensified his dislike. "I heard excellent performances of *Tannhäuser* and *Lohengrin* [he said], but Wagner's art failed to interest me, and no one could persuade me to hear the other operas."

During the next years, Sibelius, in a very productive vein, continued to develop his gifts. Ideas came readily to him, and between then and the turn of the century he wrote a large number of the works that now appear most frequently on concert programs and have contributed more than all the rest, perhaps, to his international fame.

In 1897 he also received outward evidence of the esteem felt for his art in his native land. After the first performance of *Kullervo,* voices were raised in the press urging that the young composer be accorded a public grant so that he could relinquish his teaching activities, which took up much of his time and interfered greatly with his creative work. But nothing came of the suggestion until after the first performance of the *Lemminkäinen Suite*. The Imperial Senate then granted him an annual state stipend of a couple of thousand marks, a considerable sum in those days, yet not enough to relieve him altogether of the unproductive work incident to earning a living. He could only definitely resign his position at the Academy of Music at the beginning of the new century, but the stipend enabled him to give up his tedious pedagogical work.

Since in his teaching he revealed many traits characteristic of the man and the artist, we must not neglect to quote some of his pupils on the subject. "I'm a poor teacher," were his first words when young Leevi Madetoja laid a five-part fugue before him at the first lesson. But the young student's first visit to his teacher proved very rewarding in spite of this negative introduction. "It was not teaching according to traditional pedagogical methods, but consisted of short, pertinent comments. We did not discuss my fugue at any length. Instead, we turned at once to questions of musical aesthetics. Even today I still remember some good and ever useful advice I received at that first lesson. 'No dead notes! Every note must be alive!' Can any better advice be given to a music student? The thing that distinguished Sibelius' teaching [said Madetoja in conclusion] was that he concentrated mainly on a general musical training and stimulated the personal capabilities of the student in preference to a one-sided emphasis on narrow-minded professional points of view."

Otto Kotilainen has given a very vivid account of his

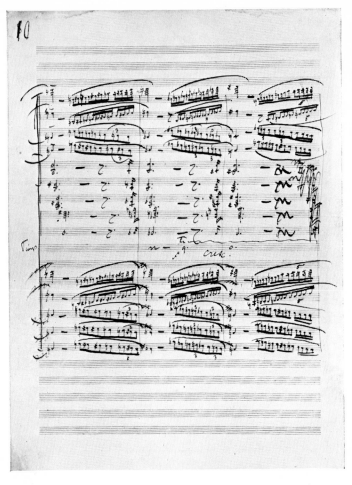

A page from the first manuscript of the First Symphony

first theory lesson at the academy. Among his classmates were two young girls who had already had several lessons. "The door opened and a tall, thin man with sparkling eyes and a thick shock of hair hurried into the room. It was our teacher. He greeted us, sat down, got up again at once, lighted a cigar, glanced out of the window, looked us over hastily, and then said to the girls: 'It's so beautiful outside. Wouldn't you like to take a little walk in the fresh air and have a look at the town?' The girls agreed to this and left, highly delighted. 'It would be a pity (he said after they had gone) if the young ladies lost their lovely rosy cheeks,' and laughed his characteristic, fascinating, jolly laugh. We then plodded this way and that through Wegelius' theory and analysis with its scales, intervals, harmonies, and distant keys which, according to the syllabus, was intended to be the teaching material for the entire year. We listened to overtones. He opened the grand piano, pressed down the sustaining pedal and banged out a low note. And we listened, all eyes and ears. 'Out in the country, I've sometimes heard overtones from a rye field as I dozed by the wayside,' he said. And I nodded to show that I believed him. During the lesson he also told us something about instruments. Among other things he asked: 'Do you play the flute?' When I said 'No,' he continued: 'The flute lies, and the higher it goes, the more it lies.' And I believed him."

That his highly unconventional teaching methods were perhaps not altogether ideal for the average student or those not overly gifted is very probable. But for young musicians who had passed the elementary stage and possessed a receptive intelligence, they must have been all the more stimulating. For Sibelius, as Madetoja also pointed out, has the rare ability to give pregnant expression to his thoughts. "Just a figure of speech that strikes the nail on the head, as it were, and everything is clearer than if a long lecture had been held on the subject." Bengt von Törne, who as a young man had the benefit of Sibelius' counsel in compositional and artistic problems, also mentions, in his work on the Master, his modest and intelligent teaching methods.

The time that Sibelius could spare for composition was very industriously employed and resulted in a large number of lyrical compositions as well as new orchestral works. Even in the lyrical works of this period one recognizes traits that reveal in his music an increased subjectiveness—a tendency that was to remove him gradually farther and farther from the more or less realistic treatment of the mythical or historical material of his youth. Without the romantic basis undergoing a recognizable change in the beginning, the composer's spiritual register widened as time went on and allowed his idiom to strive after a greater universality. In this developmental process the First Symphony represents both an end and a beginning. On the other hand, however, the period just before the turn of the century also marked the pinnacle of his creative work along patriotic lines.

In the incidental music to Adolf Paul's drama *King Christian II,* which was composed in two *étapes,* 1897-98, Sibelius' lyricism blossoms in warm orchestral colors of captivating melodic beauty. The concert suite that derives from this is extraordinarily popular. The most nationally characteristic piece of all, *The Fool's Song of the Spider (Sången om korsspindeln),* was not included in the suite but was published separately as an independent work.

The increasing inwardness and the emphasis on the personal which appeared in his lyrical production during the latter half of the nineties is reflected in his external life. Among other things this period marked the end of the Symposium. Gallen had gone abroad, and Sibelius had struck out on more personal paths of his own. The heightened subjectivity in his artistic creation, however, did not mean that he had turned his back definitely on the Kalevala and the historical or patriotic material that had captivated his imagination more than anything else during the last decade of the century. The First Symphony still contains much of the archaic mood, of the rich colors and the somber pathos of the Kalevala; but the work still moves (without any programmatic basis) on a purely subjective-psychological plane. In this respect it forms a synthesis of what has been and of what is in process of becoming.

A very systematic and methodical, but overly imaginative musicologist in Finland recently undertook to draw up a ridiculously detailed literary program for all Sibelius' symphonies (which the creator himself expressly designates as unprogrammatic) based on a large collection of leitmotifs that he himself sorted out and labeled, but which Sibelius has never recognized. However, one must categorically reject an analysis based on such personal "musical visions" that pretends to recognize in the First Symphony "Kullervo's tragedy"; in the Second, "Finland's struggle for political liberty"; in the Third, "God's nearness to mankind"; in the Fourth, the question "Where is happiness?"; in the Fifth, a "northern spring"; in the Sixth, a "northern summer"; and in the Seventh, "harvest time."

If the emphatic "No" with which the Master reacted

to my question regarding the aforementioned *Lemminkäinen* motifs were not enough to remove every vestige of a doubt concerning his artistic intentions, his attitude to the leitmotif technique and to all literary or programmatic musical creation, then his comment to an English visitor, Walter Legge, in 1934, should at all events do so. "My symphonies [he said] are music that has been conceived and worked out as musical expression without the slightest literary basis. I'm not a literary musician. For me, music begins where the word leaves off. A scene can be expressed in a painting, a drama in words. A symphony should be music first and last. Naturally I've sometimes found that an image springs quite involuntarily to my mind in connection with a musical movement that I've written; but the seed corn and the fructification of my symphonies were purely musical. When I wrote symphonic poems, the situation was naturally different. *Tapiola, Pohjola's Daughter, Lemminkäinen,* and *The Swan of Tuonela* are inspirations from our national epic. But I never pretended that they should be regarded as symphonies."

Sibelius conceived *Kullervo* and *Lemminkäinen* as an enraptured observer, as someone who experiences personally and intensively the fantastic dream world peopled by mythical figures and interwoven with enchanting moods, which he was able to translate into sound. In the First Symphony, on the other hand, the listener no longer meets with a hero from the dark past of the sagas, but Sibelius himself, his own nature, his pathetic self-assertion, his yearning, his melancholy, and his own independence of spirit. However, the archaisms still to be found in his musical idiom show us that something of his earlier manner of identifying himself with the legendary figures of his youth is still inherent in him. But now in reverse order, it is the subject, the creative artist himself, who is unconsciously influenced by the archaic atmosphere and has perhaps also taken on the nature of his former objects, the ancient heroes of mythical lore.

It does not seem to us farfetched to associate the elegiac introductory clarinet melody, accompanied only by a drum roll, with a mood of solitude, with a vision of a barren, lonely landscape from which, in the following energetic *allegro,* the promulgator of these tones suddenly springs forward himself and begins to speak with the bravado and the longings of youth and its now melancholy, now overly joyous pathos, and maintains this mood until the last bar of the symphony has faded. The only thing in the entire work that really gives the impression of an objective portrayal of mood is just this melody with its burden of solitude and loneliness.

EXAMPLE 7

As a thematic idea it is not so isolated as Cecil Gray would have us think. But even if, as motif, it were thematically fruitful for the further development (of which Sibelius himself was apparently unconscious), this melody—from the standpoint of expression—seems to have nothing in common with the rest, either here or in the introduction to the last movement where it reappears in

59

a powerful, broad orchestration. Everything else is a revealing in sound of the soul of the vision, untranslatable in literary or naturalistic language—something that can be characterized only in psychological or purely technical terms.

As far as psychological terminology is concerned, it is naturally much safer to proceed with caution. With every analyst, be he ever so estimable or sagacious, it takes a more or less subjective coloring. A good example of how an essentially sharply profiled theme is interpreted by different commentators (each of whom has something pertinent to say in his way about the character of the theme in general) is offered by the first subject of the initial movement of the First Symphony, which begins thus:

EXAMPLE 8

Let us now cull a choice bouquet of the qualities attributed to this theme. Gray characterizes it as "lithe, springing, and vigorous"; to Madetoja it is "frothing with dramatic pathos"; then we have "sharp as a sword," "penetrating," "high spirited," "defiant," "striving for freedom." Probably none of these expressions defines the real character of the theme. Something halfway between would perhaps strike it better. But this is not so easy to formulate, and it must therefore be left to each individual to find, according to his way of thinking, the most pertinent expression, in so far as that is really necessary.

What I wished to show by this illustration of the various descriptive possibilities and the emphasis on their subjective coloring was to express a reservation with respect to the psychological attributes that I myself cannot avoid employing in my description. Each one of them is open to discussion; they lay no claim to objective infallibility.

It also strikes me as a questionable procedure from another point of view for an analyst to pick out in a short passage some one motif that happens to employ the same intervals as that of another composer, and then draw rash conclusions from this. In a recent English work on Sibelius, the author, for example, likens the aforementioned first subject of the initial movement to an *adagio* theme by Borodin, which happens to follow the same melodic outline but through its rhythm and its tempo, its harmony and orchestration expresses something entirely different. Moreover in the present instance, one can dismiss all such speculations with Sibelius' simple statement that, when he wrote his First Symphony, he had never heard the work of the famous Russian.

Furthermore, however one may characterize the first subject, it is decidedly rhythmical and represents a fruitful contrast to the melodious second subject in the further development of the movement. This second subject begins as shown in Example 9.

Here the young composer exhibits an astounding artistic and technical maturity, not only in the invention and development of this theme, so fertile and pregnant with symphonic possibilities, but also in the masterly, and throughout inspired, transitions.

EXAMPLE 9

In the intensely fervent second movement, elegiac and idyllic sections alternate, rising then to an impassioned climax and concluding with the tranquil mood of the beginning. The very rough, harshly rhythmical *scherzo,* with a delicate and graceful trio, forms not only an admirably balanced counterweight to the preceding *andante,* but also a necessary slackening of the basically tragic mood of the work, which reaches its culmination in the intensely dramatic last movement.

The solo clarinet passage from the first movement, reintroduced in a powerful unisonal passage of the strings against the heavy brass, also serves—in the introduction to the finale—to outline the background of the spiritual drama of the movement. Through its instrumental, rhythmical, and harmonic intensification, it now seems heavy and pregnant with fate, and thus seems to foreshadow the pathetic *(patetiska)* conflicts and strong contrasts that characterize the continuation. Here the thematic contrasts are more striking for the strenuous development in the finale and more suited for effective dramatic climaxes than in the first movement. The movement is entitled *Quasi una fantasia,* but it very clearly has the character of a rondo. A briefly outlined rhythmical motif and the melodic variations evolved from it

EXAMPLE 10

along with the theme that completes the main group

EXAMPLE 11

form the counterweight to a broad *cantabile ed espressivo* melody for the massed violins playing on the G string.

EXAMPLE 12

The impassioned finale is evolved mainly from this thematic material and represents both psychologically and musically a great emotionally eruptive counterpiece to the first movement. Besides the introductory melody common to both movements we also find other points of resemblance at the opposite end, namely the two abrupt *pizzicato* chords with which each movement concludes.

The symphony was played for the first time on April

26, 1899, at a concert of the Helsinki Philharmonic Orchestra in a program of the Master's works and received a tremendous ovation.

The chapter in Finland's political history, known today as the "years of passive resistance," when the Russian autocrats trespassed more and more on the constitutional rights of the country, began in the late nineties. In Bobrikow, the Grand Duchy of Finland had received a governor who exposed with brutal unscrupulousness the whole extent of his pan-Slavic plan of attack. The illegal conscription and the so-called February Manifest had shaken the foundation of that legal order guaranteed by former Russian monarchs. Bitterness seethed among all classes of the population, and was reflected especially in the as yet ungagged press.

The *Song of the Athenians* was the war song that Sibelius offered as his first contribution towards strengthening the national self-confidence of his countrymen. In its mixture of Hellenic simplicity and its aggressive, steely tone of patriotism, this musical setting of Rydberg's classic verses has always been an inspiring exhortation to the public spirit in a country that has had more than its share of calamity and oppression.

During the summer of 1899 it was the free press that was principally made to feel the displeasure of the Russian overlords. One paper after the other was silenced for shorter or longer periods. In these circumstances, the thought of giving patriotic demonstrations for Finland's constitutional rights in the form of fetes in aid to the Press Pension Fund found enthusiastic supporters throughout the country. The climax of these press celebrations in Helsinki was a gala performance in the Swedish Theatre, the principal number on the program being a series of "Tableaux from the Past" *("Scènes histori-ques")*. The music that Sibelius wrote for these "living pictures" comprised an overture to the entire series, an introduction to each tableau, a soft accompaniment to the spoken text, and a concluding tone poem. The music did not come into its own until after he had revised and adapted it for concert performance. The first suite, *Scènes historiques,* which comprised three numbers: *All'overtura, Scène,* and *Festivo,* was ready at the turn of the century while the second, with *The Chase, Love Song,* and *At the Drawbridge* only received its revised, definitive form twelve years later. Nowadays we can only wonder how the contemporary vogue of living pictures— so incomprehensible to us today—could have inspired him to write such substantial music. To later generations it seems like a series of genial little tone poems.

The most noteworthy number of this series, the con-cluding tone poem, was, however, not included in either suite. "At first, neither the critics nor the public grasped what it meant [wrote Ekman]. They only understood it when after a thorough revision it was given the title that informed the whole world that here on the Arctic Circle was a little nation fighting for its life." And this title was *Finlandia!* In Finland the work was forbidden during the years of unrest, and in the other parts of the empire it could not be played under any title that revealed its patriotic character. When Sibelius appeared as guest conductor in the principal cities of the Baltic Provinces in 1904, he had to call it *Impromptu;* and in the other Scandinavian countries it was first entitled *Suomi.* In Germany it was known as *Das Vaterland* and in Paris *La patrie.*

The fermenting, threatening mood of the first motif of the work (the second), with its rich, sonorous harmonies, seems to represent the irresistible forward movement of oppressed elementary forces. Sublime in conception, the hymn, in its religious atmosphere, appears in contrast "as a fervent prayer, free of all oratorical pathos and hackneyed musical blazonry, borne by the idealism of the newborn passive resistance." (Frosterus).

By this time, Sibelius, now thirty-four years old, had attained a unique position in his own country, where he was regarded as one of its most distinguished culture bearers and greatest artists. We are unable to judge to what extent the political conditions and his active participation in the struggle for Finland's independence contributed to this, but we may go so far as to say that his intrepid art would by no means have been accepted so readily by wide circles of the public if the political conditions and the part he personally played in the patriotic awakening had not worked in his favor.

As regards the important creations of the last years of the century, Flodin, the young artist's most severe critic, also changed his tune. "Of course I know that presuppositions are necessary for a complete understanding of Sibelius' music," he wrote in 1900 in his work *Finnish Musicians*. "It took years before I myself was able to do unreserved justice to this wildly beautiful music, so full of surprises and subjective conceits of every kind. But though I still am not unreservedly enthusiastic over the composer's earlier works, I nevertheless am a warm and glowing admirer of his more recent compositions and assert that anyone can understand them who is capable of enthusiasm for, and of being moved by, really original music written by an original mind. He is not only Finland's greatest and so far only composer of genius, but as regards the great qualities of a composer, he is the most distinguished poet anywhere who writes in music—all countries included. It is really high time that his best work should be known beyond the frontiers of our own land."

The same year that this was written, energetic efforts were initiated to introduce the young master's art abroad. After it was decided that Finland should be represented at the Paris Exposition in the field of architecture and the plastic arts, musical circles proposed that the nation's young music be also included on this historic occasion. A request for a public grant was naturally turned down, but since it was considered extremely important for political reasons that music be represented and bear witness to the vitality and originality of Finnish culture, a fund was collected from private sources sufficient to cover the expenses of the proposed European tour of the Helsinki Philharmonic Orchestra, with the Paris Exposition as the ultimate goal. The moving spirit behind the enterprise was Robert Kajanus, who also conducted the two concerts, Sibelius going along as assistant conductor. Surrounding his First Symphony, as the principal item on the program, were the following works: *Finlandia,* the *King Christian Suite,* the two Kalevala legends, *The Swan of Tuonela* and *The Return of Lemminkäinen,* along with orchestral compositions by Kajanus and Armas Järnefelt and romances by Ernst Mielck, Oskar Merikanto, and Järnefelt, interpreted by Aino Ackté, Maikki Järnefelt, and Ida Ekman, the country's finest soloists.

On July 1 and 2, the "Paris Tour of the Philharmonic Orchestra" gave its farewell concerts in Helsinki and the

following day set forth on a journey that led over Stockholm, Oslo, Göteborg, Malmö, Copenhagen, Lübeck,
Hamburg, Berlin, Amsterdam, Rotterdam, and Brussels to the French capital, the terminal station. The
tournée proved to be a veritable triumphal procession for
Finland's young music and its representatives. In Scandinavia, especially, the applause amounted to an ovation,
and in the cities of central Europe the reception was also
very enthusiastic, the critics being practically unanimous
in acknowledging Sibelius' original gifts, while the Paris
papers brought particularly fulsome panegyrics. In view
of the political situation in Finland, which was well
known to the rest of Europe, one can quite well ask to
what extent this homage was influenced perhaps by extra-
musical reactions. But there was unquestionably great
sympathy for the artists as representatives of the oppressed nation.

The autumn following the successful Paris tour,
which was the first *étape* on Sibelius' path to international fame, he went abroad again and remained away
throughout the ensuing winter during which time he
made a number of contacts that were to be of the greatest
importance in introducing his works abroad. In Berlin
he met Otto Lessmann, who was extremely enthusiastic
over the young composer's art and saw to it that *The
Swan of Tuonela* and *The Return of Lemminkäinen*
were included in the program of the forthcoming festival of the Allgemeine Deutsche Musikverein in Heidelberg. In February, Sibelius and his family left for Italy
where in beautiful Rapallo he began work on his Second
Symphony. On the way home he chanced to meet Anton
Dvořák in Prague, who made a very sympathetic impression on him.

The Heidelberg Festival took place in June, and since it had been arranged that Sibelius should conduct his Kalevala legends, he had only a short time at home.

The thirty-seventh festival of the Musikverein comprised five large concerts in Heidelberg and a gala performance in the Court Theatre in Karlsruhe, the programs consisting preponderantly of new works conducted by the composers themselves, while the audience was composed almost exclusively of professional musicians from Germany and abroad. "My position as a foreigner among a crowd of eminent and influential German composers was no easy one [Sibelius told Ekman]. Apart from the general rehearsal on the day of the performance I was only allowed one single rehearsal for works that in spirit and style were quite strange to German musicians. At the first rehearsal everything went wrong, and at the general rehearsal things did not go much better on the whole. If in addition one considers that everybody was tortured and irritated by having to work in the intolerable heat (80 degrees in the shade), one will understand that I looked forward to the combined performances of the orchestra and myself at the concert with considerable anxiety."

Apart from a couple of minor blunders at the performance (according to a contemporary report) the works proved effective and made a deep impression. "The music was new and original [wrote Sibelius' enthusiastic friend, Adolf Paul]. It was fresh and independent, genial and brilliant in its treatment and above all there was nothing decadent about it. Sibelius was recalled several times with tumultuous applause and complimented by a throng of celebrities. The critics nodded in approval and seemed pleased, while old Lessmann was moved and proud at the same time. Hermann Wolff (the well-known concert manager) at once fixed a date for a Sibelius concert during the next season in Berlin." The Nestor of Finnish musicians, Professor Richard Faltin, reported a little more objectively, perhaps, that "Sibelius in spite of many adverse circumstances scored a great success. His position [he asserted] was not an easy one between Strauss, whom the orchestra greeted with a threefold fanfare and at whose appearance the audience rose to its feet—and Wagner. Furthermore, we had been listening to music for over three hours in a truly tropical heat! Sibelius was recalled twice—a success that was doubly impressive in view of the unfavorable circumstances already mentioned."

Sibelius also looked back with pleasure on the Heidelberg Festival. "It contributed greatly to making my music known in Germany, and I was surprised at the friendliness and cordiality that was shown me everywhere. The things I remember in particular were my conversations with Richard Strauss, who was greatly in demand during the entire festival. He was extraordinarily courteous to me and spoke very frankly regarding his works and his aims. I was also tremendously pleased that the divergence in our points of view in artistic matters represented no obstacle to a mutually trustful personal relationship. Later I also had evidence of his impartiality and loyalty towards my art, for which I cannot be grateful enough."

By this time his economic situation had so far improved that he felt that he could relinquish his teaching and devote himself exclusively to composition. On his return from Heidelberg, he settled for the rest of the summer in Lovisa and then during the autumn moved to Kervo, about an hour's ride by train from Helsinki, where he directed all his energies to the completion of the Second Symphony. Before the year was out, the work was finished and was played for the first time at a concert of his compositions on March 8, 1902. The concert was such a great success that it had to be immediately repeated three times in succession. Flodin's enthusiasm now knew no bounds. "We have never before heard a composition like Jean Sibelius' Second Symphony. We have scarcely ever heard anything comparable to it in the genre of the modern symphony, and the oftener one hears this highly gifted work, the more one is impressed with its contours, the more profound seems its spiritual content, and the more pregnant the bases offered for the proper understanding of the composition."

The Second Symphony announces a change of direction to this extent: the archaic atmosphere, which marked the Kalevala material of the nineties and was also found in some degree in the First Symphony, has entirely disappeared. The subjectivity now seems fully developed and provides a clear and adequate picture of the Master himself, his nature, his thoughts and moods at a time when his more or less romantic youthful period was drawing to a close. The imaginative interpretations of this work that endeavor to associate it directly with the patriotic struggle against the Russian oppressors seem to have as little foundation as those that viewed the First Symphony in a similar light.

As regards their principal structural features, the two symphonies are very closely allied, but in comparison with the more introspective minor tonality of the First, the mood of the major tonality of the Second seems positively expansive. Martial fervor and passion are common to both works and to many commentators the pathos and intensity found in them is suggestive of Tchaikovsky. With respect to the subjectivity and a number of stylistic details, it is difficult to deny a certain Tchaikovsky influence in the First Symphony; but as Frosterus points out, "the intellectual climate shows few points of contact, contrarieties apart. Where Tchaikovsky ended as a symphonist, resigned to fate, Sibelius begins with opposite indications. Where Sibelius seeks to master his own nature in purgatory and soul turmoils, the Slavic poet riots in intoxication of the senses and sensitiveness. A descending line runs through Tchaikovsky's Sixth Symphony with its abrupt changes of mood and bravado, its exaggerated emotional crises and stark brutality *(på helspann)* in spite of its enchanting Slavic charm. The remorseful resignation as conclusive result of a hunger for life is so filled with sighs and moans in the finale that the pain is morally oppressive in its realism. As overly sensual as is the Russian's frankness, just so controlled (in spite of passion) is Sibelius' self-probing. Firmly and steadfastly he holds the inner conflicts in equipoise—an artistic trial of strength that he carries out with a steady hand. Sibelius' musical nervous strength knows no collapse and no retreat. Unconquerable, he holds every inch of ground, ever stronger and more steeled for new struggles. An undeviating conclusion after a surmounted developmental stage."

Even if in the Second Symphony the Kalevala moods give way to a more individual and at the same time more universal mode of expression, it would be erroneous to think that Sibelius has thereby severed connections with his former inspirational sources. One of these—and one of the most important—is his ability (already fantastically developed during childhood and then steadfastly maintained throughout his life) to observe nature, combined with the capacity to transmute imaginatively into music the impressions thus received. His inner kinship with nature has nothing in common with the fashionable enthusiasm for it—as perfect a man of the world as he may be! But it is through and through nature itself. And he not only goes the way of nature itself in his objective music—from the *pizzicato Waterdrops* of his boyhood to the mature miracle of *Tapiola,* but even he himself almost seems like the embodiment of a spirit of nature, who also in the most subjective spiritual confessions, lets one hear his supernatural voice.

When we come across so-called pastoral moods or motifs in his symphonies, we have no reason to suspect a literary or programmatic naturalism. Probably it is far more just to look upon them as an essential element of his own nature and individual moods. An example of such a pastoral-like theme is found in the second subject of the first movement of the Second Symphony.

EXAMPLE 13

Another is the seemingly monotonous oboe theme in the trio of the *scherzo* section of the same symphony, which at every iteration of the *b♭* pulsates with enchanting life and taken as a whole is of unusual charm.

EXAMPLE 14

A very typical peculiarity of Sibelius' thematic treatment is a long drawn-out note followed by a sharply profiled, comparatively rapid, rhythmical figure. The aforesaid first subject of the first movement of the First Symphony and the second subject of the first movement of the Second Symphony are especially characteristic examples of this.

EXAMPLE 15

Taken as a whole, the introductory movement of the Second Symphony is clear and of lofty stature, and the melodic inspirations are simple and restrained. One hears melancholy notes also here, but they seldom get the upper hand and are stifled, as it were, in outbreaks of feeling that seem to lie between a harmless nature idyll and controlled manliness and virility.

The second movement can be justly designated as Sibelius' liquidation of the nineties. The long *pizzicato* passage in the introduction for basses and cellos still says nothing of importance. It merely maintains the tension, but leaves the question open as to what follows. Then a melody played by two bassoons above the *pizzicato* of the strings (one of the classic examples of contemporary text-

EXAMPLE 16

book rules of orchestration for the superb employment of the bassoon as a solo instrument) indicates the nature of the somber thoughts, which in the rest of the movement mount to an almost conclusive expression of pain, largely through the further development of this motif

EXAMPLE 17

and to melancholy resignation in the following

EXAMPLE 18

and to the more lyrical

EXAMPLE 19

However, the energetic manliness, purified by suffering, protests against the unrestrained lament expressed by these motifs in short, brusque replies of the bassoons, tuba, and deep strings above the threatening rhythmical thrum on the G strings of the violins.

EXAMPLE 20

The theme entrusted to the bassoons at the beginning of the movement then recurs in a passage for solo trumpet and solo flute above the quietly flowing triplets of the strings. The strange color effect in the deep register of these instruments seems to underline the theme's purification. But the conflict is not yet over. It is repeated again on an even more impassioned plane, and the curtain only begins to fall with the simple, powerful coda, the final chords of which close over the spiritual drama.

The effervescent *scherzo* springs forward in whirling triplet passages, which emerge in one voice after another, jumping from one to the next. All at once, however, this lively motion ceases. A short drum roll follows like an afterwash, and then the oboe begins the tender, inward melody that is quoted above. After a repetition of the most important thematic material from the *scherzo* and its gentle trio, a broad, powerfully enhanced bridge passage leads directly to the finale, in which the strings sound the beginning of the first subject above the crashing chords of the trombones.

EXAMPLE 21

The trumpets throw a fanfare into this:

EXAMPLE 22

and the horns reply, while the strings round out the whole.

EXAMPLE 23

With this main group, which through the firm grip of the strings, develops to an intense and homogeneous melodic line; in the resumption of the second subject after a couple of slight indications in the flutes and clarinets

EXAMPLE 24

and in the final theme thrown out by trumpets and
trombones

EXAMPLE 25

Sibelius has found musical material of great individuality and pregnant rhythm, which embodies all the pre-
requisites to raise this finale to that radiantly monumental and triumphal peroration, the effect of which is
unfailingly overwhelming.

At the Turning Point

It can be said that the Second Symphony marked the end of Sibelius' "romantic period." But this should not be taken too literally, for, as a matter of fact, his artistic course is so individual that one cannot apply to it unreservedly the ordinary stylistic descriptions. If, however, a division must be made according to established classifications, it should be with the reservation that he belongs strictly to no school, beyond what one might call the "Sibeliusian." He is neither a pronounced romanticist nor a classicist. He is both, and yet he is neither the one nor the other.

There is something called the romanticism of nature and something known as national romanticism. It can be said that to a certain extent both these cultural tendencies have represented great sources of inspiration for Sibelius. And yet it goes against the grain to call him either a romanticist of nature or a national romanticist. And why? Probably because his way of experiencing and expressing nature is not based on a more or less conscious act of the will, but on something that we have endeavored to explain as a sort of personal identification with nature and its phenomena, on a constitutional quality that makes him seem an unreflecting, eruptive child of nature —this in contrast to the romantic naturalists of the pre-

79

vious century with whom sensitiveness to the surrounding world of reality and its descriptions take place more or less deliberately and with intentional emphasis in the form of realistic musical imitation and descriptive tone painting. The difference is significant in that it rests on a psychologically correct observation.

But why not then a national romanticist? Because the music of the banner bearers of national romanticism in all lands was based principally on assembled ethnographic material which they—again deliberately and intentionally—worked up in their compositions. Sibelius never made use of such material. In *Kullervo* he created what one called the "Finnish style" in music before he had ever heard the Finnish runic songs. He sang only with his own voice, with his own musical idiom; but this idiom was Finnish, as it could not help being since he took it directly from nature, the Finnish and his own. He reproduced the voices of mythical antiquity just as unreflectingly as the things whispered in his ear by the imaginary creatures of nature. His incredibly sensitive ear for all this seems to me an integral ingredient of his genius.

And still it seems well to use the expression "romantic" in respect to his creations from *Kullervo* to the Second Symphony. For not only is the general character of these works "romantic," but this is also a distinctive quality of the conscious procedure to which they owe their composition. Romanticism lay in the very air that Sibelius breathed. Romanticism reached its apogee just at this time, in the circle of his friends, in the outside world, and above all in the storm and stress of youth. Youthful vitality and enthusiasm, passionate pathos, and intense emotions, an exuberant but at the same time extremely sensitive full-bloodedness—for the time being more or less externalized—all this characterized the man and his work at this period.

But we must examine a branch of his creative work that has not yet been considered—namely, his lyrical and epic works in small form. This completes the picture.

In the chips that fell from the Master's table while he fought his way from one large symphonic work to the next, we also find, as far as style and musical idiom are concerned, the individuality that made his greater creations the epoch-making works they are. His works in smaller form are all on the plane that lies between the lyrical, the epic, and the dramatic. Viewed individually, they furnish an analytical picture of the spiritual components whose sum total constitutes the most important trait in the artist's physiognomy: the symphonist. The symphonies represent the synthesis, all the other works, however, separate elements of those spiritual impulses that together form the criterion of symphonic art: dramatic contrasts, epic scope, and lyrical sensitiveness.

Even in his earliest youth, Sibelius, along with super-sensitiveness to all the harmonies of nature, had a distinct leaning towards highly dramatic phantasizing. The naturalistic lyricism of the boy of ten in *Waterdrops* had, about the same time, its realistic epic counterpart in a fantasy on *Aunt Evelina's Life in Music*.

A contemporary parallel phenomenon to the historical living pictures that were so much in vogue at the turn of the century was the general predilection for combining recitation with music. Sibelius in his youth also had a fondness for melodrama, and we have many compositions from his pen in this genre. Even though they are not among his important artistic works, their composition and their style are still of psychological interest. In one of them, at least, the musical ideas are powerful enough to stand alone even without a text. For example, large parts of the melodrama *Nights of Jealousy,* dating from the end of the eighties, have been taken over into the two last *Impromptus for Pianoforte* (Op. 5) and the melodramatic music that he wrote at the beginning of the nineties to Rydberg's poem "The Spirit of the Woods" was worked up a few years later into a balladesque symphonic work for orchestra. Parts of the *Karelia Suite* and the *Scènes historiques* also have obviously melodramatic tasks in connection with the living pictures. After the (at least outwardly) tremendously effective *Snöfrid* (by Rydberg) in 1900, which Sibelius called an "Improvisation for Recitation, Chorus, and Orchestra," he seems to have had no further interest in melodrama as an expressive form.

But the epic line based on a literary text did not end with this. In many ballad-like vocal works, which, in contrast to the preponderantly Swedish lyrics, were based preferably on mythological or patriotic material and Finnish texts (from the Kalevala or the Kanteletar), he combined with a vocal line that follows closely the poetic intention of the words a noticeably heightened intensity. The instrumental background is pictorial, and an archaic strain is at times apparent in the intervals and rhythms. To this class belong the whimsical paraphrase *Venematka,* for male chorus, and the ballad *The Ferryman's Brides* for baritone, or mezzo-soprano, and orchestra, both dating from the nineties; the effervescent and vivacious description of *The Origin of Fire* for baritone, male chorus, and orchestra from the first years of the new century, the ballad *The Captive Queen* dating from 1906, which has no national atmosphere, and *Luonnotar (Vir-*

gin of the Air), a tone poem for soprano and orchestra from 1913 that contains passages of the purest lyricism and is one of the most demanding tasks a singer can choose. With his hundred or more songs for solo voice, of which about eighty are set to Swedish texts, Sibelius has enriched song literature with a large number of the finest works, which have also contributed greatly to his international renown. The majority of these songs, whose fascinating originality ranks them among the most treasurable pearls of Scandinavian vocal music, were all written in his youth.

His first work to be published separately (1892) was a collection of seven songs by Runeberg of which *Spring is Flying,* in particular, with its sophisticated contrasts and the strongly evocative moods of both voice and piano parts, is a very great favorite. And in the little masterpiece *Enticement* (to a text by Tavaststjerna) published in a later collection, Sibelius has brought to sheer perfection in short lyrical form, his fresh, fragrant description of nature. And still the two first collections represent merely the prelude to the rich lyrical compositions whose profusion only became apparent towards the end of the nineties.

The three song collections published at the turn of the century contain one celebrated repertory number after another. Furuhjelm called attention to the remarkable coincidence that this period of tremendous lyric effusion was simultaneous with what he called Sibelius' "subjective awakening," that is, the period before the composition of the First Symphony. The later songs are, in general, more richly differentiated than the earlier ones and the composer reveals himself here in quite a different way, affording us a glimpse into his inner life not only through his choice of poems, but through the musical form in which he vests them.

The piano accompaniments alone of these new songs could furnish the material for an extensive study. A highly personal form of symbolistic composition is here combined with a strangely expressive vocal part. There is no empty decoration in the accompaniments, no external miniature painting. All is a rarely powerful realism, painted in broad brush strokes, which gives completely adequate musical expression to the poet's moods.

It is difficult to find a counterpart to such a fitting and inspired realism produced with such incredibly simple resources as we find in *Sigh Sedges Sigh*. The melancholy mood of *Black Roses* represents a striking example of the "subjective awakening" in Sibelius' lyrical creations. *The Diamond on the March Snow, The First Kiss, And I questioned then no further, But my Bird is long in homing,* and many others are also among the consummate inspirations, moved by a deep personal feeling, that the Master wrote around this time.

On a more strictly objective but equally individualistic plane, we have such sensitive poetic works as *The Tryst, Tennis at Trianon,* and others. The collections written after 1902 have new aims. They strive for a more moderate and transparent style, such, for instance, as *On a Balcony by the Sea* and *Autumn Evening,* to mention only two of them.

We cannot go further into Sibelius' rich lyrical output; it is so large that to deal with it at length and in detail would require volumes. And still we have not yet touched on the instrumental and the many *a cappella* choral works. Naturally all his lyrical works in small form are not of equal excellence. There are many things that seem to have been written more or less for special occasions and that are neither especially important nor representative.

Especially popular are the six-part songs for male voices *a cappella* set to Finnish texts from the Kalevala, the Kanteletar, and Aleksis Kivi, which are contained in Op. 18. In Finland they are justly considered classical works for male quartet. It is also interesting to note that the very beautiful suite for string orchestra, *The Lover,* was originally conceived for male chorus. A wonderful work of glowing passion and thrilling intensity is *Malinconia* for cello and piano, which deserves the attention of virtuoso cellists more than heretofore. Among the piano works we would only mention the *Kyllikki Suite,* which in structure and musical texture *(klangbild)* is— in spite of its title—a programless idyllic composition of lyrical delicacy. The C Major *Romance* and the *Canzonetta* for string orchestra are among the best known of Sibelius' small instrumental works dating from the beginning of the century, though they have never attained the same popularity as the well-known *Valse triste,* which was originally composed for the drama *Death* by his brother-in-law, Arvid Järnefelt.

After the great success of his Second Symphony in Finland and Sweden (Stockholm, 1903) Sibelius underwent a spiritual transformation that today one may say represented, on the whole, the end of the storm and stress period of his youth and early manhood.

During a visit to Berlin in the spring of 1902, he made the acquaintance of Arthur Nikisch, the influential conductor of the Berlin Philharmonic Orchestra, who the year before had already begun to manifest an interest in his music and had expressed the intention of performing

The Swan of Tuonela. Yet when Sibelius went to see him and showed him some of his new compositions, he found him strangely altered. "I had a feeling that people had been intriguing against me [he said] and this proved to be the case. I can still remember one of my German friends trying to console me by saying, 'My friend, now that they're beginning to intrigue against you, you can take it that your abilities are fully recognized!' " Felix Weingartner, on the other hand, received him in a very friendly manner, asked him to leave the score of his Second Symphony with him so that he could study it more carefully, and then promised to send it on to Breitkopf & Härtel who were going to publish it.

In the early summer Sibelius returned to Finland, where longing for the sea induced him to settle for a time in Tvärminne (east of Hangö). Here among other things he wrote *Was It a Dream?*, one of his most beautiful works, and the two aforementioned songs, *On a Balcony by the Sea* and *Autumn Evening*. In the autumn he moved to Helsinki, where he and his family spent the winter.

The youthful moods of obstinacy, profound depression, and high spirits now gave way to new questions and problems that life put to him. He began to look at things more and more from a personal and spiritual angle. True, he might feel lonely and misunderstood, but on the other hand he felt strengthened, and inward experiences awaited him that opened up to him new and fruitful paths of development. If he now forced himself to abandon fields that had already been explored and tilled, the road he took promised him something more than easily attained success.

The Second Symphony marked, in a certain way, the

beginning of a new direction, but it was not until the Third that his symphonic style developed what one might call a classical simplicity and economy of expression at the expense of romantic luxuriance and passion.

Along with the spiritual change that preceded the composition of this work, came a longing for a change of environment. Experience had taught him that only out in the country or in a real metropolis could he find the tranquillity and concentration essential for his art. "I had to get away from Helsinki [he said]. My art required another milieu. In Helsinki all musical inspiration was throttled. In addition I was too sociable by nature to be able to refuse invitations and engagements that interfered with my work. I found it very hard to say no. I simply had to get away."

Compared with the fruitful years at the turn of the century, the two winters 1902–1904 were relatively unproductive. And in the spring of 1904, Sibelius definitely made up his mind to move out into the country. He bought some property in Järvenpää, a village in Tuulusa commune on the five-mile-long Lake Tuusula[1] and the architect Lars Sonck, drew up the plans for the house. The practical and economic problems connected with the project confronted him with many dilemmas, but he was nevertheless in a happy and optimistic mood. "The house has a stone foundation and five tiers of logs," he wrote later in the spring to a friend. "If it were only finished! I fight for it tooth and nail! I long for peace and quietness. And to be able to work without worry."

The construction proceeded rapidly. Sibelius and his family took up their quarters for the summer with a peasant in the vicinity so that he could superintend the

[1] Twenty miles north-northeast of Helsinki.

work, and in September, 1904, his villa "Ainola" was ready for occupancy. In this way he found the secluded nest that he knew was a *sine qua non* for his creative work, a retreat where, in a simple and homelike milieu, he still lives and pursues his artistic interests. On September 21 he concluded a letter with the laconic statement: "Have begun my Third Symphony."

In the summer of 1903 he completed the first version of his violin concerto, which he rewrote two years later. After the first performance of the original version by the violinist Victor Novacek, Flodin was again critical. "It is quite clear [he wrote] that the composer did not want to write the sort of violin concerto that is nothing else than a symphonic work with an *obligato* solo violin. He well knew the fate of these modern concertos; once played and then discarded. Under these circumstances he preferred the other alternative: to let the soloist be the sovereign master the whole time and incidentally develop all the traditional pomp and circumstance. But in so doing he ran into the compact mass of everything that has been said, written, and composed before him. It was impossible to invent anything really new! And the vessel stranded on these hidden rocks." True, the critic did not deny that the work in the hands of a great virtuoso "might possibly be endowed with entirely new and fresh interest." But he found that "this at most would be to the advantage of the virtuoso element, not to the violin concerto as a whole, Victor Novacek's musically efficient and creditable, though technically very debatable, interpretation having given an adequate idea of the negative side of the work."

The concerto is undeniably full of hidden rocks, but these lie in the channel of the soloist, not of the composer.

If the vessel really stranded before Flodin's eyes, then this was either because it was not in the right hands, or the critic was the victim of an illusion. Even if it was not rigged for its maiden voyage like the revised 1905 model, the course was still the same, and the "compact mass of everything that had been said, written, and composed before" lay some distance outside the channel.

The concerto in its layout is a very virtuoso work, but the remarkable thing about it is that in spite of this, there is scarcely a detail that could be called an "acrobatic end" in itself in the traditional sense. Here it is only a lively delight in playing that discharges itself in wild bravura *gambades,* but these also always have their *raison d'être* and their importance in the musical picture in its entirety, which possesses both profundity and amplitude in build. The romantic idiom of the nineties is still slightly evident in the first and last movements, but brilliance and verve are essential features of the work's necessarily external nature, and it follows from this that the slow second movement is the only one offering opportunities for a deep emotional effect. That under these circumstances and in view of the—on the whole—traditionally classical form of the work, Sibelius still succeeded in imparting to the first movement a strong touch of fresh, personal, and original lyricism must inspire almost as much admiration as the clarified, profound, and individual flux of the *adagio*. The brilliant finale forms a radiant and—for the soloist—extremely grateful close.[2]

2 One hears this movement interpreted very differently at times. Some soloists take it very rapidly, others like a polonaise. When I asked the Master about the correct tempo, he replied: "It must be played with sovereign control—rapidly, of course, but not so rapidly that one is not always in 'perfect command.'" Sibelius never gives exact tempo indications when questioned on this point. He believes that one can rely

In 1905, Sibelius' works were performed in several important musical centers abroad. In January he was called to Berlin to conduct his Second Symphony in Busoni's "Modern Music" series. The performance was an unquestionable success, the press extraordinarily friendly. The critic of the *National Zeitung* was indignant that he had not heard the symphony before and felt that it was the "duty of Nikisch or Weingartner to let Berlin hear such a work."

About this time Toscanini's attention was also drawn to Sibelius, and he conducted the Second Symphony, *Finlandia,* and *The Swan of Tuonela* with the Scala orchestra. "Since then Toscanini has shown a gratifying interest in my music," he said and then told how the Italian maestro, after performing the Fourth Symphony in New York early in 1930 without very great success, played it three times in succession so as to hammer it thoroughly into the consciousness of the bewildered public.

In the autumn a revised and final version of the violin concerto had its baptism of fire at a Singakademie concert in Berlin with Karl Halir as soloist and Richard Strauss conducting. According to Sibelius, Strauss put the orchestra through three rehearsals, a fact he stressed to show how conscientiously Strauss prepared the works of other contemporary composers.

Sibelius went to England for the first time in 1903 (not in 1905, as Ekman states) where he conducted the First Symphony and the *King Christian Suite* in Liverpool and Manchester. Even then he could notice that the

---

on a good artist's intuition to find the correct nuances within the tempo indications provided by the note values and does not wish to place any additional restraint on the interpretation.

English had understanding for certain characteristic features of his music that the contemporary German critics rejected as mere eccentricities. A second journey to Great Britain, originally planned for the spring of 1905, could not take place until the autumn, soon after the first performance of the violin concerto in Berlin. This time he conducted (among other things) his Second Symphony in London.

He was received in England with unstinted cordiality. In the beginning he was the guest of the composer Granville Bantock at his country house in Birmingham, where (he said) "I enjoyed such true English hospitality that I never got acquainted with English currency!" In London, Sir Henry Wood took great interest in him and through this conductor he met many persons who later were tireless champions of his music in England, among them Mrs. Rosa Newmarch and Ernest Newman. After he had made arrangements for other performances of his compositions and had signed engagements to conduct his own works, he went on to Paris, where he found that here too his name, as a composer, was well known. The Lamoureux Orchestra had recently played *The Swan of Tuonela* and other works were announced for future programs of the orchestra.

In January, 1906, he returned to Finland, stimulated by new impressions and with many new plans awaiting realization. He was wholly engrossed with his Third Symphony, and in addition had promised to write the incidental music for *Belshazar's Feast,* a play by his friend Hjalmar Procopé, which was to be given in the near future. Finally the Kalevala had given him a new inspiration, namely, episodes connected with Väinämöinen's wooing of the Daughter of the North, entitled *Pohjola's Daughter*.[3]

During the previous year he had completed some exceedingly important incidental music for Maeterlinck's play *Pélleas et Mélisande*. Here as in the incidental music to August Strindberg's fairy tale *Svanehvit (Swanwhite)*, written some years later, he demonstrated his rare ability to evoke, with few resources, a subtle and fascinating mood of faery. The suites for concert use, which were put together from the music to these plays, are far superior to the occasion for which they were originally written. Gossamery poetry of highly individual coloring speaks from each of these small musical gems. The music to *Belshazar's Feast* seems much lighter in comparison, although it enjoys unvarying popularity. Here Sibelius employs an archaic idiom in exotic local color that reminds one of Grieg's *Peer Gynt Suite*. But as clever and as accurately aimed as were his effects, and as great the evidence of his musical many-sidedness, the artistic content is not up to that of his other incidental music, including the *Valse triste*, which, on the whole, is an extremely inspired piece of music.

Pohjola's Daughter, a tone poem dedicated to Robert Kajanus and called in the score a "Symphonic Fantasia," was completed in the autumn and performed for the first

3 (Trans. note.) "The poem attached to the score is a paraphrase of an episode which recounts how Väinämöinen, also on his way back from the Northland, comes suddenly upon the maiden of Pohjola, seated aloft upon a shining rainbow, spinning. Enchanted by her radiant beauty he beseeches her to come down to him and join him, which she refuses to do except on condition that he will, by means of his magic arts, make for her a boat out of the pieces of her spindle. Väinämöinen toils in vain, unable to discover the correct magical formula, until finally in despair he relinquishes his attempt, and leaping back into his sleigh, continues his homeward journey." (Gray.)

time shortly before Christmas in Petrograd under the direction of the composer. With this work Sibelius shows that he was not altogether untrue—for the sake of his subjective symphonic credo—to the sources that had been such a great inspiration to him in his youth. But his style is now entirely different. In the objective, realistic portrayal of old Väinämöinen's unsuccessful wooing of the Daughter of the Northland, seated upon a rainbow, one finds much that in mood and coloring seems more related to the impressionistic tone poems of more recent date than to those inspired by the Kalevala.

Still we find in it many traces of earlier influences. This is program music since it entails not only atmospheric but also pictorial connotations—as in *Lemminkäinen in Tuonela* and *The Return of Lemminkäinen*. In thematic treatment and structure there are many points of contact with the legends of the nineties—for example, in the development of the initial solo cello motif, from which proceeds the *ostinato* sixteenth-note figuration portraying the rhythm of Väinämöinen's sleigh ride, and in the puissant and defiant motif of the horns that terminates the main group and seems to have a certain psychological relationship with the tremendous chords of the horns that symbolize Lemminkäinen's death struggle in the whirlpools of the Tuoni River.

During all this time Sibelius was working indefatigably on his Third Symphony, although with his uncompromising self-criticism, his progress was fairly slow. He had already received a flattering invitation from the Royal Philharmonic Society to conduct the first performance of the work in London in March, 1907. But he was obliged to postpone the journey since the work was not yet ready. In the summer he put the finishing touches to the score. The first performance then took place in Helsinki on September 25, and during the winter he also conducted the work at a concert in Moscow.

With the Third Symphony he struck out on an entirely different path than in the first two, a new orientation, already augured in earlier works. At the expense of romance and pathos, his symphonic style develops to an ever purer classical simplicity and economy of expressive resources. Even from the purely external aspect, the Third Symphony differs from its two forerunners in restraint in the employment of the orchestral forces and in concentration of form. If in the first two symphonies, the wind, and especially the heavy brass, predominated, now the strings take precedence. In the Third there is very little of the eruptive passion of the first two symphonies. Expressive and coloristic intentions have receded into the background in an effort to achieve a quiet and controlled but brilliant scale of colors. The moods breathe clarity and light. The motifs seem to exhale the fragrance of country idylls.

The thematic material is extraordinarily clear and easy to grasp. The first movement, which starts off at once with the first subject in the cellos and basses, is so promising in its rhythmical tensions and its melodic simplicity that it immediately arrests the hearer's attention,

EXAMPLE 26

to capture it completely in the following phrases that round it out:

94

EXAMPLE 27

In spite of its very limited melodic amplitude, the second subject (presented by the cellos in its authentic form) has also a strangely thrilling effect because of its inherent developmental possibilities, which in the continuation are utilized for both figurative and melodic expression.

EXAMPLE 28

The second movement is one of the simplest symphonic movements that Sibelius ever wrote. Fundamentally it consists of little else than colorfully orchestrated variations of the following figures given out by two flutes:

EXAMPLE 29

At the beginning of the finale, we find several disjointed and in themselves insignificant little melodic figures which gradually are welded together into a logical and coherent tissue. It would lead us too far to analyze this arresting development in greater detail; so we shall limit ourselves to closing this short description of the most important thematic material of the Third Symphony by quoting the march-like theme introduced by the violas divided between the four voices, which forms the center of gravity in the second closing section of the finale:

EXAMPLE 30

One may ask, "Is there anything more lucid and more harmonious, more purely classical and clearer than the themes here quoted?" And when we hear the work, we find that its symphonic treatment is always a true development of the energies latent in it.

V

Voces intimae

In November, 1907, the public of Helsinki enjoyed a memorable guest performance of the conductor Gustav Mahler, who conducted works by Beethoven and Wagner. Sibelius tells us that during Mahler's visit, he saw him on a number of occasions. "Contact between us was established in some walks during which we discussed all the great questions of music very thoroughly from every angle. When our conversation touched on the nature of the symphony, I said that I admired its style and severity of form and the profound logic that created an inner connection between all the motifs. This was my experience in the course of my creative work. Mahler's opinion was just the opposite. 'No! [he said]. The symphony must be like the world. It must be all-embracing.'"

The conception of the nature of the symphony formulated here by Sibelius and of the inner, logical connection between its motifs is not only extremely noteworthy and characteristic of his conception of art, but it is especially important when one considers that its background was the two great works that he was planning at this time and in which the unity and consistency of style and idea reached their highest perfection.

If we study Sibelius' creative output up to his fortieth year, we find that with all his obstinate individualism and its sensitive passion, there is a certain lack of inwardness. At any rate the Third Symphony and the violin concerto, with their classically clear form and their dampening of the pathos of the youthful works, quite clearly indicate a change of direction to a more mature self-mastery. But still it was not until the string quartet *Voces intimae* and the Fourth Symphony that he turned away from external phenomena, became more than ever introspective, listened in his creative work to the innermost voices in his soul, and gave them utterance with a subtle reserve and a spiritualized beauty that seems to penetrate to greater emotional depths than anything that he had written heretofore.

When he began a string quartet in 1908, he returned to a genre that he had neglected for two whole decades in favor of the rich color scale of the orchestra and the direct unfoldment of his wonderful lyric gift. In conformity with the new psychological course of his development, he sought the expressive means that accorded best with the ascetic sublimation process undergone by his world of musical ideas.

That the spiritual change reflected in the string quartet and the Fourth Symphony is connected in a way with the inner crisis through which the Master passed during these years, is quite apparent. But it is not within our province to seek to fathom its real nature. We must only attribute it to something spiritually deeper than the serious throat malady that perhaps occasionally upset his equilibrium and resulted in a painful operation and the prohibition to smoke cigars; or to the economic worries that continued to cast a shadow over his existence. He himself only referred very briefly to the crisis in a letter to an intimate friend when he remarked laconically—

"I've suffered and learned much." But what he did not say in words, he expressed in music.

The string quartet *Voces intimae* was completed during the winter of 1909 while he was in London, he having finally accepted the invitation of the Philharmonic Society, extended to him the year before, to conduct his Third Symphony. On his fourth visit he strengthened his friendly ties and extended his acquaintance with prominent English musicians, among them Rosa Newmarch (who even before the turn of the century had been an enthusiastic admirer of his art) and Mary Wakefield, at that time an excellent singer who in later years placed herself and her wealth wholly in the service of far-reaching musical aims. While there he also met Claude Debussy and Vincent d'Indy, who happened to be in London at this time. "My English friends showed me much attention [he said]. I was invited out a great deal and enjoyed it very much, although I was not allowed to touch either wine or cigars. I also heard a lot of new music—Elgar's new symphony, Bantock's *Omar Khayyam,* Debussy's new songs and his orchestral suite *Nocturnes*—all most interesting music. Everything I heard strengthened my conviction regarding the path I had chosen and the one I must follow in the future."

Thus it was amid the turmoil of a great city that he wrote the one work that is farthest removed from the tumult of the world—just as two decades before he had written his G minor quintet in Berlin and had demonstrated even then that his creative ideas were proof against ephemeral external impressions and that he too was impervious to the effect of his environment.

In its formal structure the string quartet departs from the traditional four-movement type, but it is not unique in this respect. Beethoven in his last quartets made similar departures, and Haydn wrote his first quartets with two minuets, one before and one after the slow movement. One can say that the five movements of *Voces intimae* are reminiscent, to a certain extent, of Haydn's arrangement, as Gray also brought out. The introductory movement has definitely the character of a "first movement," the last is a typical finale, and the slow middle movement is framed by two movements, each of which—in a very original way—bears the stamp of a *scherzo*. The position of the slow middle movement, as the work's center of gravity, is underlined through this symmetrically balanced "pyramidal" movement plan. The first violin and the cello sound a gloomy, meditative note right in the introductory dialogue.

EXAMPLE 31

The *Allegro molto moderato,* which follows immediately, completes the main theme group of the movement in orthodox sonata form with:

EXAMPLE 32

and several cello phrases related to the introduction and accompanied by an *ostinato* violin figuration. The second subject, which enters after a transition, brings contrasting material:

EXAMPLE 33

The development is comparatively short and is built, primarily, on the motifs of the principal group, and the recapitulation—as so often with Sibelius—is a striking modification of the exposition. The coda leads directly to the second movement of the quartet, which is unique among Sibelius' compositions in that it employs material derived exclusively from the previous movement. One might actually call it a *scherzo* treatment of the second subjects of the first movement. Although, in structure, the development of the first motif is very free, its relationship to the second part of the above-quoted second subject (see bar 5 of Ex. 33) is perfectly clear:

EXAMPLE 34

and we also find an agreement almost note for note in the

101

further progress of the movement, which recurs repeatedly at different pitches and is finally identical, note for note, with the original version. (See bars 2–6, Ex. 33). The thematic treatment that these movements share in common also seems to have led to the direction to play them right through without interruption, an assumption confirmed by Sibelius.

EXAMPLE 35

The *adagio* is not alone the formal center of gravity of the entire work, but its ethereal beauty and the com-

EXAMPLE 36

In the studio of Wäinö Aaltonen, 1935
Photo Pietinen

Villa Ainola

Jean Sibelius in his garden, 1947
Photo Bryan

bination of expressive power and quiet reverie in its
melodic line entitle us to call it, as well, the psychological
climax of the quartet and to seek therein the key (but
not in the sense of program music!) to the colloquy of
the "inner voices," the *voces intimae*. There is something
of an endless melody in the melodic line of Ex. 36. And
after a two-bar phrase—in canonic imitation, rare
enough with Sibelius—which is a fragment of the above-
quoted melody, there follow three transcendentally mysterious E minor chords

EXAMPLE 37

that quite involuntarily evoke the feeling of their having
turned a key in a lock so as to open to our senses a world
of transcendental wonder. (In a miniature score of the
quartet belonging to one of Sibelius' friends, I found
this interpretation in a penciled note by Sibelius himself. He had written the words *voces intimae* over these
three chords.

It is futile to attempt to give even a faint idea of the
further course of this movement. Its immaterial musical
substance is clearly shown in the musical examples. It

may only be added that the three mysterious chords (now in C sharp minor) return again as introduction to the coda. Here it seems as though the key were carefully reversed in the lock to prepare us for an awakening to reality.

But the reality that now confronts us is not yet the trivial world around us. The music goes further and it is the heavy, concretely materialized first subject of the fourth movement that draws our thoughts more to the earthly-obvious.

EXAMPLE 38

But it is not in the nature of this sublime music to let us tarry long in the realm of the earth-earthy. After a repetition of this theme, the continuation diverts our thoughts to other things. If we carefully examine the bars in the preceding movement that immediately follow the three E minor chords—the *voces intimae*—our attention is drawn to a couple of little phrases that play no important role in the *adagio,* but anticipate an important theme of the fourth movement, treated here in sequence. Against the background of the triplets in the middle voices, this motif gives the second and—in comparison with the first—far more serious *scherzo* its rhythmical swing.

EXAMPLE 39

A third motif, which is a little more spun out and also much more rounded off, is the following:

EXAMPLE 40

The movement develops this thematic material and employs formatively the peculiar timbres of the four instruments by having them enter singly or simultaneously with the others, while a characteristic combination of fragments of the first subject with an anticipation of the triplet movement of the second brings the movement to a close.

The fifth movement is a lively, forward-moving, energy-laden, free rondo of typically finale character in which a transparently orchestrated *spiccato* figure and

arpeggios underline the "motion" and the following
sharply outlined and essentially Sibeliusian motif plays
the leading thematic role:

EXAMPLE 41

The rhythmic incisiveness and vivacity of this finale
make it a well-balanced closing movement for a work of
whose inexhaustible wealth of profound and spontan-
eously original ideas it is impossible to give more than a
superficial idea in words and musical examples. One
must actually hear it and experience it in its entirety,
preferably more than once. For it not only stands, but actually demands, repeated hearings, and each time charms
and convinces the hearer more and more.

"The more abstract the tracks become on which a
musical work moves, the more superfluous seems the
verbal description that shuns objective analysis [wrote
Sigurd Frosterus]. As regards Sibelius' Fourth Symphony
in A minor, that most chaste and delicate work reflecting
his emotional life during a questioning, uncertain period
of transition, a respectful silence were perhaps the best.
The cloud-like mental images that he here transmutes

into music are so vague that the traditional portrayal by means of concrete figures would be inadequate. There is not a single theme that rings out sonorously or waxes in volume, not an idea that takes tangible shape. The ever-alert disinclination to give definite form to continually fleeting ideas can neither be carried farther nor be more conscientiously observed. But this skittish reaction towards the undefinable is counterbalanced by a wide-open receptivity to evanescent impressions—airy wraiths from all over hovering midway between sleep and reverie."

In their penetrating and concise formulation, Frosterus' words show clearly the fundamental nature of this ascetic work, which was written a couple of years after the string quartet and could perhaps with equal right be entitled *Voces intimae*.

In the spring of 1910, Sibelius began the new symphony, which was to take such a commanding position among his works. At a time when the banner bearers of Russia's pan-Slavic expansion policy, despite all protests of the civilized world of Europe, adopted "Finis Finlandiae!" as their slogan, Sibelius anxiously watched the alarming developments, but kept his feelings to himself and avoided all fruitless theoretical speculations. "I've always hated all empty talk on political questions [he said], all amateurish dabbling in politics. I've tried to make my contribution in another way."

His thoughts were entirely taken up with the symphony. The slowly maturing score accompanied him on all his travels; when he conducted his works in Norway in October, 1910, when he went from there to Berlin and Leipzig, and finally in February, 1911, when he left on a concert tour to Göteborg, Riga, and Libau with a detour to Berlin. On his return to Finland the work was finished.

In contradistinction to the bright mood of the Third Symphony, the prevailing atmosphere of the Fourth is one of brooding gloom, while its formal structure is as elusive and baffling as the Third is simple and clear. In place of the self-contained, plain diatonic themes of the earlier work, we find for the most part in the Fourth pregnant thematic germs only, a strange and decidedly free treatment of the tonality principle, dislocated rhythms, and frequent syncopations. The scoring is almost spare in texture, and the absence of all sensuous charm (Elmer Diktonius called it very aptly the "Crust Symphony") coupled with the great concentration it demands in the listener resulted in a lack of appreciation in wide circles, though according to Cecil Gray, "for the few it probably constitutes—with the Seventh—Sibelius's greatest achievement."

In speaking of the Fourth Symphony, Gray quotes a passage from Thomas Hardy's *The Return of the Native* to the effect that "the time seems near, if it has not actually arrived, when the chastened sublimity of a moor, a sea, or a mountain will be all of nature that is absolutely in keeping with the moods of the more thinking among mankind. And ultimately, to the commonest tourist, spots like Iceland may become what the vineyards and myrtle-gardens of South Europe are to him now; and Heidelberg and Baden be passed unheeded as he hastens from the Alps to the sand-dunes of Scheveningen." Gray adds that the "change forecast by Hardy in this prescient passage has already come about, not only as regards our feeling for nature but for art as well. There are already a few who find greater pleasure in the moor, sea, moun-

tains, sand-dunes and even the gaunt wastes of the Fourth
Symphony than in the more mellow, opulent and super-
ficially attractive soundscapes of other composers."

As an example of compression and the elimination
of superfluities, the first movement of the Fourth Symphony is without parallel in symphonic literature. It is
furthermore unusual in being a slow movement. The
initial four notes embracing the compass of an augmented
fourth constitute the principal thematic germ of the entire symphony.

EXAMPLE 42

The real first subject introduced in the seventh bar
of the movement by a solo cello over a tough battle between the notes *e* and *f*♯ in the basses illustrates in another
way the fundamental mood of loneliness and brooding
melancholy.

EXAMPLE 43

The *f*♯ eventually gains the upper hand and leads—
according to traditional concepts—from the original key
to the remote tonality of which it is the tonic. A melodic

figure (evolved from the introductory motif) in the higher strings over somber, menacing harmonies of the brass
effects a daring modulation and at the same time pro-
pounds the second subject of the movement.

EXAMPLE 44

After a modified and intensified version of this strenuous theme, the mood, heavy with conflict, gives way for
a moment to a radiant shaft of sunlight; idyllic horn fan-
fares sound a B Major chord that disperses all the black
clouds. But the sky once more darkens and the exposition
concludes with a soft closing group consisting of the two
principal subjects. The development begins with a
strangely fascinating passage introduced by a solo cello,
which culminates in the highest registers of the violins,
to descend again to a *tremolo* passage that leaves the real
thematic action to the woodwinds and deeper strings.
This strange, unisonal, unaccompanied development is
composed of a cello phrase of the principal subject and
the syncopated motif of the second subject.

The little figure given out by the woodwinds over the
tremolo passage for strings can be identified as the characteristic augmented fourth (really octave plus fourth)
of the second subject. The phrases of the woodwinds become flickering little figures, and scattered drum rolls
underline the menacing mood, which culminates in a
climax leading to the greatly reduced recapitulation. In
the coda we again find the short, slow phrase of the introduction, which is now raised a third. Then, in rising

EXAMPLE 45

octave imitations (i.e., from one group of strings to another) it finally dies away on a long held *a*.

This concise description of the first movement of
the Fourth Symphony agrees in all essentials with Eino
Roiha's analysis, which views it as a free treatment of the
sonata form. However, if we look more carefully at the
thematic material and its treatment, we find very little
left of the psychological antitheses that characterize, for

example, the layout of the classical Viennese sonata
with its thematic contrasts. The continuous augmented
fourths and the syncopated rhythm in the introduction
and the second subject give them a distinctly inner relationship. The conflict between the notes *e* and *f*♯, which
begins in the syncopation of the introduction, continues
all the way through as fundament for the first subject
given out by the solo cello, and the closing group com-
prises both the motif of the introduction and that of the
first subject. A fundamental thematic unity therefore
runs through the *entire* exposition and continues consequently through the whole movement. But despite this—
and this is one of the marvels of Sibelius' genial handling
of the motifs—the movement offers an astounding wealth
of contrasting ideas, rapidly fleeting moods, colors, and
emotional values which fills us with amazement at the
Master's ability to work such wonders with so little. The
tone poem *Tapiola* dating from the twenties is another
example of it.

However, the augmented fourth not only plays an
important role in the first movement but dominates the
thematic material of the entire symphony. In this way,
Sibelius succeeds in establishing a unity of mood and
thought between the different movements without,
moreover, impairing their thematic independence. In

EXAMPLE 46

the oboe melody that introduces the second movement,
the interval makes only a transient appearance.

On the other hand it is very pronounced in the following
graceful play between the oboe and the violins:

EXAMPLE 47

In the following passage in dactylic metre, which ex-
tends for about forty bars, one can already analyze note
for note a couple of figures that after a short dance-like
flute interlude and a repetition of the introductory section, enter in the following form, which is almost dramatically enhanced by a strong accentuation of the augmented fourth:

EXAMPLE 48

The last bars form an amazingly simple and modest
synopsis of the most important motifs of the rondo-like
movement.

In the groping woodwind introduction of the slow
third movement, we find the characteristic interval of
the symphony again in the notes forming the first phrase:

EXAMPLE 49

A more emphatic and purposeful idea is very soon given out by the horns, although it does not seem to be fully developed as yet. As so often with Sibelius, here fragmentary motifs are employed, which are gradually built up until when the time comes, a full sized theme arrives. And this is only found in its finished form towards the end of the movement, in the shape of a powerful melody of the strings:

EXAMPLE 50

The soft coda employs a previous major variant of the first subject. Right after the full-toned string melody, we note a self-contained bar in the third movement whose only task is to prepare the coda. The same phrase introduces the finale, but in that movement also it has no developmental function as such. Contrary to Cecil Gray's premature conclusion that it forms only an isolated introductory motif, we find notwithstanding that its final variant in the repetition is nothing less than the germ cell for the important augmented fourth, triplet-like motif of the violas thrown out almost like an imitation.

EXAMPLE 51

Moreover this final rondo also represents an example of Sibelius' typical symphonic technique of throwing in small melodic fragments and motifs, which then gradually develop to a firm organic theme. They are treated with astounding tonal, rhythmic, and instrumental subtlety and are so combined as to produce with these modest resources highly individual tonal alloys and evoke moods and impressions as from a distant metaphysical world.

We now ask how the Helsinki public reacted to this daringly linear, transcendental wonder. "I still recall very vividly the first, and to a certain extent, very curious first performance [wrote Furuhjelm], the head shakings, the doubtful looks, the harsh or ironic judgments, and the not quite first-rate performance (the symphony is not one of the easiest to perform), which explains why it did not meet with greater success. However, in spite of all their skepticism, the Helsinki public displayed, as usual, great considerateness. Our more progressive western neighbor presented a companion piece to the Helsinki performance wherein whistles provided the actual finale." The critics, in general, were also greatly undecided, but it would be unjust to conceal the fact that there were also far-seeing persons who appreciated the symphony.

The critic of a leading Helsinki paper could only interpret the symphony as program music, associating it with a pleasure trip to Koli that Sibelius and his brother-in-law Eero Järnefelt had made a few years earlier. Movement by movement he tried to show what aspects of nature Sibelius—in his opinion—was trying to depict. Entirely contrary to his custom, Sibelius could not refrain this time from registering a laconic but indignant public protest against the tendency to seek a programmatic basis for experiences of an introspective, psychical nature, although naturally he did not wholly deny that, in general, impressions of nature had always been for him a great source of inspiration or that there was some connection between this symphony and the stimulating Koli experiences, which is indirectly indicated by his dedicating the work (probably not altogether accidentally) to Eero Järnefelt.

V I

Impressionistic Harmonies

It is a ticklish matter to apply to another genre of art such stylistic designations as "impressionism" which were originally employed only for painting. It also seems to me that they are often applied much too summarily and arbitrarily to musical works, with the result that ordinary salon music as well as a "refined" romantic naturalism are in many instances unjustifiably characterized as impressionistic music. I shall therefore preface my employment of this term with a few explanatory remarks to show the importance I attribute to this concept.

The concept "impressionism" is derived from the word "impression." Impressionistic art strives—even though by technically different means—to reproduce the impression either of external phenomena (nature and scenery) or of subjective impressions, fantasies, and visions. The vague, indefinite style of typical impressionism is (at least in the province of painting) to be understood as a reaction against orthodox naturalism. The discovery that a color can be conceived as an independent light impression and has none of the ordinary qualities of a phenomenon, forms the basis of impressionistic painting which, contrary to the traditional idea that a tree is green and the sky blue, asserts that colors may be quite different in different lights and different atmospheres.

Like the painter, the impressionistic composer, for example, conceives a chord primarily as a sound impression, as an independent sound phenomenon in contradistinction to the traditional manner of viewing harmonies as partial functions within the major-minor tonalities. The impressionistic artist avoids an obvious portrayal of reality; he dissolves the sharp contours and merely indicates the vague atmosphere surrounding the object he desires to reproduce or portray.

Strictly speaking, musical impressionism in consummate form has only one representative—the Frenchman, Claude Debussy. Presages of the special manner he evolved can, of course, be found in his countryman Berlioz and the Russian, Mussorgski. Yet what Debussy created was in its way entirely new. In his works we find no real handling of motifs. With him there is seldom anything that grows thematically or undergoes development; but we marvel at his mastery in rendering dreamy, passive moods and fleeting, restrained emotions by means of a sophisticated melodic line and the vague harmonies of a refined color chart charged with rich sonorities.

How far is one now justified in calling Sibelius an impressionist? In any case one must not apply the term to the realistic Kalevala symphonic poems of his youth, even though one seems to recognize in the atmosphere of the details a certain natural lightness in capturing mental images and expressing them in colors. "Clearly pictorial as is Sibelius' youthful style [wrote Frosterus] no greater mistake can be made (as has so often happened) than to call it impressionistic. Few clichés are more misused (namely, retroactively) . . . . One can scarcely imagine a sharper contrast than that between Debussy, three years older and pioneer of the conscious musical impressionism, and Sibelius, when they both set Maeterlinck's play *Pélleas et Mélisande* to music. Sibelius' atmospheric background swallows neither action nor structure. Debussy embroiders in pearl grey in disintegrating the colors, and resolves the scenes in chromatic vibrations."

In contradistinction to the conscious impressionist, Sibelius never felt the need to protest or fight against naturalism, or react to it at all. Being the positive and in no way reactionary personality that he is, he has never, to my knowledge, proclaimed any definite stylistic program, either impressionism or any other trend. He has never abnegated the ideal of his youth, its national idealism and mythological realism. And therefore he could never be an impressionist *pur sang*, although he did not hesitate to avail himself of the stylistic resources of impressionism or to interpret subtle impressions in an essentially imaginative but often enough half-naturalistic context.

With a fondness for a luxuriant and colorful orchestral palette, which from the very beginning he employed with an original technique of his own, he has always had a deep respect for thematic treatment and its essential importance *(cerebrala betydelse)* in a musical work. Whatever coloristic extravagances he may permit himself, the logical and structurally correct handling of motifs always forms a backbone that gives his works stability and stature. An early example of this is the symphonic poem *En Saga* where the clear thematic layout and the strict treatment of the form, combined with a fantastic and sparkling orchestral color (the impressionistic moods of the saga vision) produce an "active" effect that carries one along with it, which is diametrically opposed to the "passive" indolence of a Debussy tone poem where the effect rests predominantly on the sophisticated perfuming of the orchestral and tonal compositional treatment.

One can no more call Mussorgski or Berlioz an impressionist than the younger Sibelius. But as one can say that the two first composers anticipated many of the stylistic resources of impressionism, so too it can be said that Sibelius used them already in his youth quite intuitively, even though their employment was limited to the outer layers of the realistic conception and they had not, as yet, left their definite stamp on the musical substance of these tone poems.

Without disavowing the tone poems of his youth, Sibelius, in several orchestral works dating from this century, has nevertheless approached very closely to the typical impressionistic ideals as regards delicate evocation of mood. The first blossom of this type is the dance intermezzo *Pan and Echo* from 1906 (revised in 1909), a brisk, fragrant forest idyll of enchanting charm.

Although bearing an earlier opus number (Op. 45) than *Pan and Echo* (Op. 53), *The Dryads,* "a gay, floating leaf from the woods" (in the words of Elmer Diktonius) was written in 1910. A contemporary critic wrote that "here Sibelius had achieved something in a sphere regarded till then as the domain of the new French masters" and that he had drawn an atmospheric picture of the dryads dancing and frolicing in the protection of the grove with as "sophisticated a clarity and coloring as only a Debussy could have done."

In keeping with the impressionistic character of this little tone poem, the thematic material is very sparse. Only demure, delicate motifs of a bar or two, a mysterious chord, or a little waltz fragment. That is all. Yet the vision of the timid play of the dryads in the enchanted wood is portrayed with an almost incredible sensitiveness and finesse in the employment of the coloristic, harmonic, and rhythmic resources of impressionism that lay ready to the Master's hand.

In *Night Ride and Sunrise,* completed in 1909, one is tempted to speak of a synthesis (in music perhaps less than in painting) of the antithetic concepts naturalism and impressionism. Yet here this apparently paradoxical combination is not valid for the composition as a whole. Formally it falls into two parts. The first depicts the night ride; the second, the sunrise. A gallop, which in reality produces strong, rhythmical sounds, lends itself for this very reason to a naturalistic portrayal in music. But not so a sunrise. Here there is rhythm too, but one cannot perceive it audibly. If it is to be rendered in music, it is done by portraying mental images (visionary impressions).

If the galloping trochaic metre of the first part, which goes on uninterruptedly in many different melodic lines for over three hundred bars, represents the naturalistic element of the composition, then the little ascending phrase of the piccolo flute and the bass clarinet, which seems to symbolize the first faint ray of light, introduces the fascinating episode that depicts, with unsurpassed mastery of the resources of musical impressionism, the dawn of a northern sunrise where the light breaks through slowly and intensively and banishes the darkness of night.

One of the least known but most noteworthy of the symphonic poems is *The Bard,* which was completed in 1913. The relationship it bears to the Fourth Symphony, that profound masterpiece of his middle period, is akin (as Gray points out) to that existing between *Tapiola* and the Seventh Symphony, which crowned his later period in a similar manner.

The Bard has no other program than that implied by the title, and its character in general is dark and brooding, almost rhapsodic. In order to obviate misunderstanding, it is well to point out that here it is not a question of the great bards of the Kalevala saga, of the eternal singer Väinämöinen, as Ernst Tanzberger for example, claims; but the title, according to the Master himself, refers to a "bard in the ancient Scandinavian sense and milieu."

In only very few of Sibelius' works is the thematic material so thin and incorporeal as here. In the first of the two sections of the work, there is scarcely anything that can be called a theme—harp chords accompanying long drawn-out cello harmonies and delicate string passages, a small figured passage for muted violas and bass clarinets, and finally a somber little melody in the violins. And nothing else. The second section resembles a shimmering impressionistic painting. One seems to catch something of the enchantment of the bard's playing; and the most prominent, relatively clear, and definite idea consists of several small syncopated woodwind phrases. These are worked out in a suggestive crescendo culminating in the only total employment of the brass in the entire work. Finally in the closing bars we hear a couple of tranquil harp chords again, reminiscent of the introduction.

In the autumn of 1911, Sibelius, after a long and very fertile period at his home, Ainola, left again on a foreign tour. "I was in Berlin in October [he said] and in Paris in November. After such a long preoccupation with my own art, I was impelled as never before to seek momentary release from myself in the concert halls. I've never listened to so much music as during those two months. I heard as much as I could, both old and new. I've always been interested in my contemporaries and younger composers—as much as anything in order to gain a clear view about myself." A letter written after a performance of a Bruckner symphony testifies to the intensity of his musical experiences. "Yesterday [he wrote] I heard Bruckner's B Major Symphony, and it moved me to tears. For a long time after I was completely enraptured. What a strangely profound spirit, formed by his religiosity! And this deep religiosity we've abolished in our own country as something no longer in harmony with our age!" A few words in another letter dating from the end of the first month of the First World War illustrates his own personal attitude towards religion. "How much pathos in our time [he wrote]. We are drawing nigh the predicted religious era. But it's impossible to define religion—at least in words. Perhaps music mirrors it."

The beginning of 1912 he received a call to the Conservatory of Vienna to take over a class in composition; but without pondering it long, he declined the flattering offer. First of all because he wished to remain in Finland, and second because his head was buzzing with ideas of his own, and he felt that he could not conscientiously accept a post that required him to devote a great deal of his time and interest to the work of his pupils.

After a summer holiday in Kuhmois during which, among other things, he revised his orchestral suite *Scènes historiques II* and wrote the first of the beautiful violin serenades (in D Major and G minor), he left for England in the autumn, where he had guest engagements in five cities. "The principal item in my program [he said] was the Fourth Symphony and I was very anxious to see how an English public would receive it. The venture was undoubtedly bold, in view of the doubtful reception it had had from the Finnish public. The English, however, proved surprisingly sympathetic. There was nowhere such a climax as in Göteborg where the first performance of the symphony was actually hissed."

After he returned home, it was first of all the very subtle and engrossing tone poems *The Bard* and *Luonnotar* (for soprano solo and orchestra) that absorbed all his attention. The second violin serenade and the music to the tragic pantomime *Scaramouche* were also written during 1913.

Towards the end of the first decade of this century, he had already heard that his music was having an extraordinary success in the United States, but in between times he also received reviews from European music centers that showed him that here his art still encountered skepticism and opposition. But this did not shake his equanimity. "I had gradually got used to having the musical press pull me to pieces day by day and to being reminded both of my good and my bad deeds. I had learned to take it calmly. I was now quite sure of my art. When I read devilishly malicious criticisms, I took it as evidence that my development was making rapid strides."

In the United States, however, his popularity waxed from year to year, and numerous American organizations had already invited him to conduct his own works. In the beginning he gratefully but firmly declined all such offers—even financially advantageous ones—since it had never interested him to make capital out of his art. If he had availed himself of the opportunities offered him in this respect, he would surely now be very rich— but not the man he really is. His rejection of the American offers was also prompted by the fear that the long voyage and the many new impressions might hamper his productivity during the intensely fruitful creative period through which he was then passing. But in the autumn of 1913 he was at last willing to consider an extraordinarily flattering offer from the United States.

A wealthy American, Carl Stoeckel, for many years director and conductor of the distinguished and exclusive Norfolk Festival, which had numbered among its former participants such celebrities as Dvořák, Saint-Saëns, Bruch, and others, invited him to write a new orchestral work and to conduct it, along with some of his older works, at the forthcoming festival in June, 1914. Mr. Stoeckel's letter showed him to be a distinguished personality with a knowledge of music, and this together with other pleasant circumstances banished the Master's scruples. He accepted the invitation and commenced work at once on the new composition. During his visit to Berlin at the turn of the year, he did not neglect the work and the following spring completed it at home in Järvenpää.

He originally intended to call this broadly conceived impressionistic description of the sea, with the enchanting play of the water nymphs in the heaving swells, *Rondo of the Waves*. With the title he ultimately gave it *(The Oceanides)* he apparently wished—leaning on the world of mythology—to underline the fact that here it was not alone a question of a realistic picture of the ocean in music, but of a desire to evoke a fantastic scene of a sea filled with living spirits of nature. "The title [he explained] has reference to Homeric mythology and not to characters in the Kalevala. The Finnish title of the work *Aalottaret* (Daughters of the Waves) is merely a translation."

Sibelius lays too much weight on the logical development of his musical ideas to let the extravagant imaginative richness with which he treats them flicker out in the empty nothingness of thematic instability. This lends his impressionism a far more personal, active quality than Debussy's, for example. A comparison of his *The Dryads* and *The Oceanides* with *L'Après-midi d'un faune* and *La mer* of the French composer (prompted automatically by the similarity of the themes) offers much of interest, but need not be gone into here, in this connection.

The Oceanides is a free but firmly constructed rondo. The sea itself with its rolling billows rises before us, in the main, in the broad sweep of the string orchestra, supported by harps and drums, while the spirited and graceful motif of the woodwinds symbolizes the play of the mermaids in the waves. It is astonishing that Sibelius was able in this symphonic poem to create such a rich variety of moods and to communicate such an intensive experience of the sea under the most divergent aspects before he himself had ever crossed the ocean. One also recalls in this connection the fact to which reference has already been made that in his youth he had found quite intuitively a specific Finnish idiom in his music before he had heard the Finnish runic singers.

His receptivity to impressions of nature seems quite miraculous. And withal it is nature itself and not salon-music artistry. There was no need to proclaim or develop impressionism as an artistic style to teach Sibelius that the ocean was not only traditionally blue-green but can also be—as he testified himself—"wine colored" or "silver grey."

Even the form in which he cast the string suite *The Lover* in 1911 (the thematic material of which harks back to a work conceived in the nineties for male chorus on a text from the Kanteletar) received a strong dash of the impressionistic coloring that the Master was fond of employing in his orchestration during the first half of the decade.

In the lyrics dating from this and still earlier periods, he also abandoned more and more the swelling melody and the realistic characterization that stamped his works of this genre at the turn of the century. The two collections of eight songs (Op. 57 and Op. 61) and the many lyrical piano works, are less gushingly exuberant than formerly. They are more restrained in style, more subjective, the texture is thinner and more transparent. A change in style appears to have taken place, having reference to the deep spiritual reflection of the *Voces intimae*—the "inner voices" in the string quartet of that name—and the Fourth Symphony with the impressionistic orchestral visions of mythical experiences of nature.

But exactly what is the relationship between the intensified, abstract world of ideas of the first-named works and the imaginative world of the others, peopled by supernatural creatures? Is there, in fact, any apart from the chronological?

A deep psychological gulf separates the two groups. The *Voces intimae* and the Fourth Symphony are fruits of that strict *subjective* conception and reflect, substantially, a solution of those problems with which the Master had been struggling in his innermost soul. The symphonic poems based on literary texts, on the contrary, are on an *objective* plane and are quite clearly associated with fantasies and mental images that floated before the Master and for whose translation into music he was a sensitive and personally participating medium.

Erik Furuhjelm—without good reason it seems to me —characterized the style of the Fourth Symphony as expressionism, and in connection therewith pointed to the dominating role played in this work by the linear extension (or melodic line) and the expressive thematic curves. But if it is difficult to apply the concept "impressionism" to music—even approximately—the term "expressionism" is far less applicable. The false analogies can be—and have been—legion. Even in Debussy's typically impressionistic works one can also point to the important role played by the melodic line and the expressive thematic curves in holding together the richly colored texture. In so far as one can point out a musical motif or melodic fragment at all, it is always a question of a curve or a melodic line. The line, as such, also cannot be denied to impressionistic music even if, at first glance, it may seem possible to do so. But under no circumstances has Sibelius' Fourth Symphony anything whatever in common with that type of musical expressionism that Arnold Schönberg and his school tried to carry through —at least up to a couple of decades ago.

In spite of the undeniable points of concurrence (in style and technique) between Sibelius' abstract, subjective symphonic treatment and the objective symphonic poems of this period, it would still be altogether unmotivated to speak in the first instance of impressionism. This stylistic term, as I have defined it, presupposes the existence of an idea that creates an impression, some aspect of nature, a mythological figure, a mental image or the like. However, the stylistic treatment of the musical material, the restrained thematic layout, the renunciation of any padding in texture and orchestration, the subtly balanced orchestral color chart from every point of view —all these are important qualities that are common to the music of *Voces intimae* and the imaginative art of the impressionistic symphonic poems.

I have in no way desired to overemphasize the impressionistic traits of Sibelius' music with these stylistic observations, but only to restrict them to the few works to which this designation really applies. Sibelius' art— viewed in broader perspective—has such a positive, synthetic universality and such an outstanding personal style, that no modish cliché is good enough to describe it.

Sibelius made ready to go to the United States. Shortly before his departure, he received evidence of the esteem that his country felt for him when the University of Helsinki invited him to be present at the ceremonies in connection with the conferring on him of the honorary degree of doctor. "I was very sorry that while accepting the honor of the invitation I had to say that I would be unable to be present in person when the degree was conferred [he said]. My promise to Mr. Stoeckel was now binding, and it would have been all the more difficult for me to go back on it at the last moment since I knew that extensive arrangements had been made to make my stay in the United States both productive and pleasant in every respect. Fortunately my Finnish friends fully appreciated my point of view."

The Atlantic crossing provided the composer of *The Oceanides* with countless new sensations. I have already intimated what the ocean's changing play of colors meant to him, and would add that he not only had beautiful weather with wonderful sunsets but variety was provided by a wind and thunder storm and the sight of a large school of "porpoises that slowly approached the ship and passed it in a playful row." There were also many other new sensations for the traveler crossing the ocean for the first time so that one can readily appreciate that it remained for him "an unforgettable memory."

Upon arrival in New York, where he was met not only by Mr. Stoeckel but a swarm of American reporters who overwhelmed him with all sorts of possible and impossible questions, it was clear to him all at once that he had "made a name" in the United States. "I was very astonished at being so well known. I should never have believed it!" he said in commenting modestly on his reception, during which he was informed that Yale University had decided to confer the honorary degree of doctor of music on him on June 19.

While in the United States, he was Mr. Stoeckel's guest at his home in the vicinity of Norfolk, Connecticut. Shortly after his arrival he had an opportunity of conducting a rehearsal of the festival orchestra and this first rehearsal filled him with the brightest hopes. "What an orchestra!" he exclaimed at the very recollection of it. "A hundred picked performers from the Boston and New York Symphony Orchestras. It was the finest orchestra I've ever conducted!" He spoke with equal warmth of the exceedingly friendly reception extended to him. "Mr. Stoeckel did his utmost to make my days pass pleasantly. His hospitality really overpowered me. I was surrounded with everything that the luxury of the American upper classes had to offer and I've never, before or since, lived such a wonderful life!"

A whole day of the festival was devoted exclusively to Sibelius and his works. The program included *Finlandia,* the First Symphony, *Pohjola's Daughter,* the *King Christian Suite,* and as an impressive finale, the new symphonic poem *The Oceanides.* When Sibelius appeared on the platform, the large audience of music lovers, professional musicians, and critics rose to its feet and the orchestra greeted him with a fanfare. The concert was a complete triumph for him. The public gave the works a tremendous ovation and the critics were no less enthusiastic.

After receiving the degree from Yale in a time-honored and impressive ceremonial in which great homage was shown to the new doctor *honoris causa* (for instance, only his music was played at the ceremony), the Master set out for home rich in new impressions and experiences. During the return voyage he and his fellow passengers received news of the fateful assassination in Sarajevo.

Three Symphonies and a Suite Champêtre

"*The outbreak* of the war was a complete surprise to me [he said]. I had never seriously imagined that the greatest nations in Europe would start a war with each other. Everyone thought at first, just as I did, that the war would not last more than three months at the most. It was therefore impossible at first to take it as tragically as the situation demanded. It would have been another matter if one could have then foreseen what years of indescribable misery it would bring with it."

After his return from the United States he received numerous proposals and commissions of various kinds, among others one for an opera based on Juhani Aho's *Juha* (a project that was carried out later by Madetoja) and a ballet on motifs from the Kalevala, which was to be performed in London. After thinking the matter over carefully, he turned the proposals down. He did not want to be a "prolific composer," as he said in a confidential letter, for this, he felt, would mean the end of his art. "Perhaps I'm too much of a hypochondriac [he added]. But to waste on a few *pas* a motif that would lend itself brilliantly to symphonic treatment!" For Sibelius himself the war had one serious effect in interrupting his connections with his German publisher whose royalties were his principal source of income. At that time Finland was not yet a party to the Bern Convention, so that he was deprived of a large part of the performance fees of his works abroad, and even much later their increased performance in the musical centers of the world brought him little material advantage. He was able to maintain connections of a sort with Breitkopf & Härtel through his Danish publisher, Wilhelm Hensen in Copenhagen, who was now publishing many of his works. And before long he also acquired a publisher in England.

During the first years of the war financial considerations forced him to write a large number of piano pieces and small works for violin and piano. Although there are many real lyrical pearls among them, they must still be largely viewed as less important occasional pieces tossed off during breathing spells when the Master, under the pressure of the exciting events of that time and the throes of his own creative work was occupied with the new symphony that had filled his mind since his return from the United States.

"The clarity at which he aims [wrote Ekman] is not easy to attain at a time of general chaos. But his intuition guides him along the right path and—even in hours of despondency and doubt—gives him insight and intuitive perception." "I wasn't sure whether I should begin the Fifth Symphony or not," he said to Ekman. "In fact I suffered a good deal through my persistence in writing symphonies at a time when practically all composers had gone over to other genres. My obstinacy became a thorn in the flesh to many critics and conductors, and opinion has only changed in recent years."[1]

[1] Ekman's book was published in 1935.

Work on the Fifth Symphony was interrupted by the production of the many small works of this period and by tours in Scandinavia during which he conducted his own compositions in Göteborg, Oslo, and Bergen twice in succession. In the autumn of 1915 the Fifth Symphony was nearing completion and was performed for the first time at a concert conducted by the Master on his fiftieth birthday, which was celebrated as a national holiday. The homage began early in the morning at the general rehearsal for the evening festival concert and continued throughout the day in the form of deputations and individual callers, reaching its climax at the festival concert, which was followed by a banquet, on which occasion leading personalities in various fields of activity in Finland combined in honoring "the country's greatest son." Even though for a full decade, Sibelius had followed other, narrower paths than those of former years— which were accessible to everybody and had brought him unqualified understanding and widespread popularity, the spontaneous homage of the entire nation on his fiftieth birthday still afforded him (in the words of Ekman) "lively evidence that in the greatness and bright calm of his maturity he possessed, as none other in the country, the love, gratitude, and admiration of his people."

The concert itself, at which the Helsinki public heard for the first time not only the Fifth Symphony but also *The Oceanides* and the two violin serenades, was a great success and had to be repeated three times running. Among the other marks of homage was a festival concert of the Helsinki Municipal Orchestra with Robert Kajanus and George Schneevoigt conducting and Ida Ekman as soloist, a singer famed far and wide as an interpreter of Sibelius' songs, a large number of which were written for her.

But Sibelius himself did not seem to be satisfied with his Fifth Symphony. In the autumn of 1916 he revised it with a "view to still greater concentration in form and content." In this revised, and as he then thought, "definite version," the work was performed by the Helsinki Municipal Orchestra on December 14, 1916. But the Master still underestimated his self-criticism, which grew more and more merciless as time went on; for the work did not receive its definite form until fully three years later.

The Fifth Symphony, as already stated, represents a quintessence of the spiritual mood or turn of mind that had dictated his creative work in the preceding years. "In this [wrote Frosterus] the Master, from the prospect of life's noontide, praises the Olympian happiness of intellectual maturity." The symphony bears very few traces of the brooding gloom and somber melancholy that constitutes the keynote of the severe and powerfully moving Fourth. It is more open, franker; and like the Third, is a transparent, richly and sonorously scored work.

As a formal creation, the first movement has given all the analysts and commentators much to think about, and they have never been able to decide whether it is to be viewed as one or two movements. There is no doubt something baffling about it, and the fact that no numerals are prefixed to the various movements in the score, as is customary, is proof that Sibelius himself never wanted to force on anyone a definite opinion on this point. Although the two sections of the first movement follow consecutively without a break, one is struck by a little detail that seems to separate the two. The letters inserted in the score for purposes of rehearsal stop short with the letter "N" and begin again with "A" at the point where the second section of the movement begins. But as Cecil Gray quite correctly points out, "this is not conclusive" (if the composer himself actually inserted the letters!) because there are not enough letters in the alphabet to carry right through in any case and sooner or later one should have had to return to "A" again. In point of fact, the whole thing is a question of terminology. The music is the same whether one regards it as one movement or two. At all events the organic relationship of the individual parts is beyond discussion and seems to foreshadow the fusing of symphonic elements, which is carried to a logical conclusion in the Seventh Symphony.[2]

In reply to my question, Sibelius stated that in view of the fact that both parts are based on the same thematic material, he regarded the whole as one movement, though he did not seek to impose this interpretation, since the second part had very clearly the character of a *scherzo*.

Irrespective of this we can see that the thematic material, consisting of fragmentary motifs with character-

EXAMPLE 52

[2] A foreshadowing of the fusion of the two movements in the Fifth Symphony is found in the first two movements of the string quartet *Voces intimae*, which are also played straight through without a break. Here too the second movement consists of material from the first, treated in the manner of a *scherzo*.

istic woodwind figures in the main group, is worked out and developed at the beginning of the first part.

In addition, there is a pregnant second subject:

EXAMPLE 53

which, after a powerful crescendo, leads to the closing theme:

EXAMPLE 54

So far everything gives the impression that here we have to do with one of the Master's typical expositions, which should normally be followed by a development and the recapitulation in order to make the sonata form quite clear and definite. But this is not the case. Instead, there follows immediately an extended recapitulation with a series of thematic variations. After this comes a section that one can take either as a development following the recapitulation, or as an extensive coda leading to the second, *scherzo*-like section of the movement. This —and rightly so it seems to me—is regarded by Toive

Haapanen as a second recapitulation, but a recapitulation that is greatly changed in character and extraordinarily free in structure. The thematic relationship with the material of the exposition supports this hypothesis and furthermore, the layout of the movement (which at the first glance seems so complicated) can be made to agree essentially with the classic disposition: exposition —recapitulation—development—repetition—coda.

The mood of the second movement (or the third, if one prefers this interpretation) resembles in some respects the corresponding movement of the Third Symphony. Against the reserved background of woodwind harmonies, the strings converse *pizzicato* with two flutes and form thereby the theme, which represents the basis of all the freely treated variations of the entire movement.

EXAMPLE 55

The harmonic background of the variations is often decidedly harsh, such, for example, as this undogmatic *(fördomsfria)* encounter of the notes *c, c♯, d,* and *e* at the beginning of the first variation:

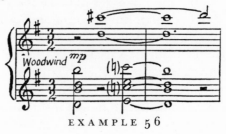

EXAMPLE 56

Furthermore a progression hidden in the double basses should be noted, which appears in two versions and foreshadows at this point a sustained motif from the finale.

EXAMPLE 57

The final movement begins with one of those long *tremolo* string passages that are such a distinctive feature of Sibelius' later symphonic style.[3] After the woodwinds have participated in the development, the horns, reinforced by the strings, introduce the motif indicated in the preceding movement in the double basses:

EXAMPLE 58

This motif gradually develops the broad character inherent in it, and in conjunction with another warm, singing woodwind theme

EXAMPLE 59

[3] This passage also makes use to a large extent of thematic material from the preceding movement. See pages 83–84 and 99–100 of the miniature score.

which is doubled by the cellos, rises finally (after an extended variant of the introduction of the movement) to a triumphant climax that, in sheer magnificence of thematic architecture, would be hard to duplicate in the entire symphonic literature.

In form, this finale (as Frosterus puts it) is "an outburst of a sorely won but full-blooded optimism, whose dynamic hopefulness almost shrieks in the disillusioned ears of the present. Superior to the tempest ranging round him, the seer follows the promptings of his own ego, yet, notwithstanding, the message that rises through the dithyrambs has in it something of a subjugated natural force. On the threshhold of a harrowing period of the war, Sibelius set up a resounding fanfare whose very first echo was stifled in the suffocating atmosphere. But the waves of the music roll on towards that clearer intellectual atmosphere that must dawn some day."

During the third winter of the war, the Russian Empire began to crack in all its joints; its tremendous army dissolved in complete chaos, which also led to portentous revolutionary changes in Finland. Even in the peaceful neighborhood of Sibelius' home, Ainola, the unrest could be noted. The murder of officers in the not far-distant garrisons as well as in Helsinki and other garrisons was a daily occurrence, and shots were heard both night and day.

In his helplessness with respect to what was going on around him, Sibelius sought in inward intercourse with virgin nature and in intense creative work a consolation for the disappointment that humanity afforded him when, as now, it succumbed wholly to its lowest instincts. But spring came again, and from this time dates a little notation in his diary, which in the brevity of its style, is like a little poem. "A wonderful day, spring and life. The earth exhales a fragrance—mutes and *fortissimo*. An extraordinary light that reminds one of an August haze."

Apart from the *Jaegermarsch,* which was composed in a few days in an exalted patriotic mood in compliance with a secret request to write something to cheer up the Finnish cavalry regiment that was being trained in Germany as the first step towards Finland's liberation, the summer and autumn were devoted exclusively to symphonic composition. The plan for a new symphony had matured, and Sibelius decided at the same time to give the Fifth Symphony a thorough and final revision.

Unfortunately Finland's declaration of independence on December 6, 1917, did not put an end to the chaotic conditions following on the Russian revolution. Rioting spread throughout the country; strikes, plundering, and murder formed the introduction to, and continued throughout, the tragic civil war that now broke out, transforming the young nation into a bloody battlefield.

In February, 1918, Sibelius was informed by the local staff of the Red forces that he was forbidden to leave the precincts of his villa. He did his best to forget the grim reality, since he was helpless to do anything about it; and sought distraction in his creative work. He entered the prohibition of the Red staff in his diary in a few words, adding in his desperation and irritation: "But what has all that got to do with a symphony?! If I could *only* get away from it all!"

Soon after this, his house was searched for hidden food supplies and weapons, and two days later was subjected to a second visit. The entries in his diary dating from this time vibrate with bitterness. However, it was not the indignation of a citizen incensed by the insolence of the champions of the lower classes, but the reaction of an artist and individualist to the brutal invasion of the sanctity of his private life. "What a shame for my house that I had to allow them to open all the drawers and see the treasures of this poor, destitute house exposed! They say that one should give way to violence. This one can do, but it is harder to bear the dishonor that befalls one's house."

His friends in Helsinki had already tried repeatedly to persuade him to move to the capital, which was presumably safer. But all these efforts were in vain. Finally Robert Kajanus arrived, escorted by two Red guards, and at last induced him and his family to come to Helsinki where they then resided with his brother Christian (head physician at the Lappviken Asylum) until the end of the war. At this time Sibelius lost forty pounds in weight due to the precarious food situation.

Towards the end of the nerve-wracking period that began with the war and ended with Finland's war of independence, the Master was filled with an overwhelming feeling of released creative power, though not to the extent of being idle. Even during the enforced residence in Helsinki in the late winter of 1918, amid the general tension and uncertainty, he composed a big cantata for chorus and orchestra *Oma maa (Our Native Land)*, which he himself called an "Ode to Finland's scenery and light nights." And yet it seemed to him as though he wanted to make up for a long period of idleness by still more work. "Ideas simply seethed in his brain [wrote Ekman]. Once again he bravely resumed the struggle to make the Fifth Symphony the ideal work he had visual-

ized. The Sixth Symphony and the plans for a Seventh
matured simultaneously." "It was as if I were prepar-
ing to quit this life and in descending into my grave shot
an eagle on the wing—taking a long, careful aim without
a thought of what was in store for me," wrote Sibelius in
a memorable private letter of May 20, 1918, which was a
wonderful and characteristic description of his frame of
mind at that time. He had always been very reserved
regarding his creative plans; but this time the letter
(which Ekman published in facsimile) contained a frank
statement of his future plans.

"My new works, partly sketched and planned. The Vth symphony in a new form—practically composed anew—I work
at daily. Movement I entirely new, movement II reminiscent
of the old; movement III reminiscent of the end of the first
movement of the old. Movement IV the old motifs, but more
effectively worked out. The whole—if I may say so—a spirited intensification to the end (climax). Triumphal. The
VIth symphony is wild and impassioned in character. Somber, with pastoral contrasts. Probably in 4 movements, with
the end rising to a somber roaring of the orchestra, in which
the main theme is drowned. The VIIth symphony. Joy of life
and *vitalité* with appassionata passages. In 3 movements—
the last a "Hellenic Rondo." All this with due reservation.
You will understand. It looks as if I should come out with all
these three symphonies at the same time. As usual, the sculp-
tural is more prominent in my music. Hence this hammer-
ing on the ethical line that takes hold of me entirely and on
which I must concentrate and hold out. . . . With regard to
symphonies VI and VII, the plans may possibly be altered,
dependent on the way the musical ideas develop. As usual
I am a slave to my themes and submit to their demands.
From all this I see how my innermost self has changed since

the days of the IV symphony. And these symphonies of mine are more in the nature of professions of faith than my other works."

These plans were realized later along entirely different lines. Still, as a document that throws light on the manner and nature of Sibelius' symphonic conception, this letter is of inestimable value, not least because it refutes psychologically—and more convincingly than long dissertations—the attempts of pedantic and imaginative analysts to interpret, by means of self-invented motto themes (leitmotifs) and their own private "visions," the symphonies of the Master as programmatic tone painting.

Fifteen years later Sibelius made the following comments to Ekman regarding the plans outlined in this letter. "The reservation in my statement about the two new symphonies was fully justified. The Fifth Symphony was not completed in its final form until the autumn of 1919, and a long time was to elapse before its two successors appeared, and then not exactly in the form I had originally envisaged. The final form of one's work is, of course, dependent on powers that are stronger than oneself. Later on, one can confirm this or that, but on the whole one is merely a tool. This wonderful logic—call it God if you will—that governs a work of art is still the conclusive factor over which one has no control."

In January, 1921, Sibelius was engaged to conduct his Fourth Symphony at a concert in Queen's Hall, London, where Busoni, the friend of his youth, was also guesting at the time. On this occasion he met for the last time the most loyal champion of his art on the continent.

Around the new year, 1923, he had guest engagements in Sweden and Norway. At the time of his departure, according to his own statements, three movements of the new symphony were completed. When he returned home the entire work was finished and on February 19 was performed for the first time in Helsinki under the direction of the composer, "the last time I conducted in my native land," he said. His first concert was at Stockholm, which also represented his first appearance in that city. From there he went on to Rome where he directed a concert in the Augusteo on March 11, and on his way back, conducted a concert of his works in Göteborg, "the city that manifested the greatest interest in my music," he said and then stressed the very positive reaction there. "I met many good friends in Göteborg, above all Wilhelm Stenhammer, who often invited me. Yes, I have countless pleasant memories of Göteborg."

A Swedish member of the orchestra when the Master conducted his works in Göteborg summed up his own impressions of Sibelius as a conductor (and, if one may believe him, the impressions of his colleagues) in the following words: "Göteborg's symphony orchestra had already played his works before, but the fact is that the orchestra, even when playing under other very good conductors, was never able to interpret Sibelius' compositions as eloquently as under the Master himself. His beat was distinct and easily grasped, his conducting clear to the finest details, and there was no difficulty in grasping his intentions. For example, I have seldom heard such delicacy of shading as under Jean Sibelius."

As regards the Sixth Symphony, Cecil Gray wrote that it is not only far less popular than the First and Second, but that even admirers of the Fourth and Seventh have little regard for it. "It falls between the stools, in fact, of the appreciation of the many and the appreciation of the few [he wrote]. The impression which it makes upon one at a first hearing is apt to be somewhat negative. It seems neither to soar to the rapturous heights of the Fifth, nor to plumb the somber depths of the Fourth; it has neither the breadth and grandeur of the first two, nor the fresh charm and sinewy, athletic grace of the Third. On close acquaintance, however, one gradually discovers in it certain individual qualities which earn for it as secure a place in one's critical estimation as is held by any one of the series."

Another English critic has also broken a lance for the unjustly neglected Sixth Symphony. Constant Lambert writes in his *Music Ho!:* "Although at present this fascinating study in half-tones, emotional and orchestral, is overshadowed by the grandeur of No. 5, I feel that future commentators may find its intimate quality more indicative of the true Sibelius, just as many of us feel that Beethoven's Fourth and Eighth Symphonies are more *echt Beethoven* than the popular odd-number symphonies." Finally Diktonius has also written some memorable words on the Sixth Symphony. He finds that it takes on easily "a religious, organ-like tone; but religion is also to be found in still forests and unruffled autumnal waters. And only God knows which religion is the best—nature's blind prayer or man's conscious adoration."

In its concentrated form and restrained scoring, we can characterize the Sixth Symphony as a midway point between the ascetic Fourth and the more expansive Fifth. The effort towards concentration finally attained its zenith in the one movement Seventh Symphony. The spiritual and emotional keynote of the Sixth consists in a sense of clarity and poise and a careful and mature avoidance of every kind of extreme. The scoring is neither opulent nor sparse, though the Master permits himself the luxury of a harp, which he had not employed since the First, and a bass clarinet, which he has not elsewhere employed at all in his symphonies. The coloring is in intermediate tones; soft, mellow lights predominate; the tempos are neither conspicuously fast nor slow; and the dynamic contrasts are never sharp or violent.

In discussing the Fourth Symphony I drew attention to the augmented fourth as the pervading keynote of the work. In the Sixth Symphony the peculiar modal atmosphere imparts a spiritual unity to the whole four movements, without one being able to establish any one theme that is directly common to all. According to Jussi Jalas, however, the fact should still be stressed that the theme from which the whole symphony organically evolves is stamped with the quality of the Dorian mode. Consequently this is the keynote of the entire work.

In addition, Jalas, in questioning Gray's statements, stresses the fact that Sibelius' use of modal effects in this work is not at all unusual. He points out that in the Master's early works, especially, one often finds melodic elements that have a modal character and that this archaism was suitable for underlining the specific Finnish-national traits in Sibelius' works. In the Sixth Symphony, however, one cannot well say that the archaic style has been employed with this idea in mind. It is interesting to note how the composer, with an essentially similar melodic line, has been able to evoke such divergent atmospheric moods as the rooted *(rotfast)* Finnish-national quality of his youthful works, and the modal atmosphere of this, which is akin to the spiritualized asceticism of a Palestrina. Jalas concurs in the opinion— in all likelihood, the correct one—that Sibelius did not adopt the modal style with deliberate intent, but that it was an organic part of his inspiration. It simply fell into his hands like other expressive resources that he employs in another connection, for example in rendering into music the sensation given by a particular scene.

The Sixth Symphony begins simply and quietly in tranquilly flowing lines, carried by the strings. Against this clear, devotional background, we hear the first version of the first subject introduced by the woodwinds.

EXAMPLE 60

A very characteristic trait in all Sibelius' later symphonic writing is the way he introduces, employs, and develops little thematic fragments consisting of passages in thirds for the woodwind. One cannot imagine any passage more unpromising at first sight as a subject for fertile symphonic development than this:

EXAMPLE 61

But subsequently it is seen that this, in the Master's

hands, is the case to a very high degree. The development that Sibelius often employs—and particularly in this work—is roughly defined by Gray as follows: "Suppose a theme to consist of several separate little phrases or recognizable features *a, b, c, d.* After introducing it, Sibelius will, on repetition, omit *a,* let us say, and substitute for it a new phrase *e;* and so on gradually and unobtrusively, almost imperceptibly, until one has a theme *e, f, g, b,* which when one refers it back, is found to be entirely different from what one started with. In the same way, in fact—or so we are told—that no single cell of one's body remains the same after seven years, and we are therefore entirely different people at the end of this period from what we were at the beginning of it, although the continuity of personality remains, so the thematic tissue of Sibelius' later style of symphonic writing similarly undergoes a ceaseless process of elimination and replacement, ever renewing, yet always preserving, the same fundamental unity and identity."

The motif in thirds quoted above also undergoes a series of such transformations in the course of the movement. But this does not mean that we have here only a series of metamorphoses of the same theme. The movement is written in the sonata form, and the main theme is followed by the second subject and the closing theme, each with melodic breadth and rhythmic precision.

The Sixth Symphony also differs from the others in that it has no slow movement. Instead, there is a lyrical *allegretto* of great melodic charm and rhythmical finesse, with a curiously melancholy gaiety. It begins with a series of syncopated harmonies for flutes and bassoons that give it a strangely faraway atmosphere. Then soon afterwards the violins propound the real theme of the movement, which forms the basis for the diverse variations of the continuation.

The lively *scherzo* movement lacks the customary trio. Instead it has a definitely rondo character, as has likewise the following finale. The trochaic metre of the theme with which the movement opens runs through the entire movement, which employs, moreover, *scherzo* ideas of typically Sibeliusian character.

Gray says very correctly that the tempo indication *Allegro molto,* as applied to the beginning of the movement, is "somewhat misleading." "Conductors [he continues] are apt to take the first bars much too fast and, in consequence, to make them sound utterly ridiculous." The clear, pregnant first subject introduces a dialogue between violins and woodwinds on the one hand, and the deep strings on the other.

EXAMPLE 62

The variant of the reply of the deep strings, propounded energetically by strings and horns and prepared with abruptly interjected phrases of sharply defined rhythm, is of great importance in the handling of the motifs in the continuation.

Gray did not succeed in finding an explanation for

Sibelius and Sir Thomas Beecham at Ainola on June
18, 1954, during the Sibelius Festival
in Helsinki, June 10–18, 1954

Photo Bertil Dahlgren

this in spite of the satisfactory effect of an apparent in-consistency in the fresh line of thought at the end of this final rondo, which in his opinion "bears no relation to anything that has gone before." Contrary to Roiha, he here failed to take into consideration Sibelius' not un-usual device of melodic inversion. What looks like a "new" motif at the first glance

EXAMPLE 63

is nothing but an inversion of the motif at the begin-ning of the movement,

EXAMPLE 64

which shows its natural organic relationship with the foregoing. The extremely beautiful preparation of the close, characterized by the entry of this motif, is, like the last bars, of sublime tranquillity, a peaceful calm be-yond the stress and strain of the everyday world.

In March, 1924, Sibelius completed the work that he first thought of calling *"Fantasia sinfonica,"* but for good reasons he dropped this title to give the work its undoubtedly more correct designation of "symphony." It was his Seventh Symphony, the parts of which form a coherent unit.

The work consists of one single long movement in which we can distinguish four definite sections. First a slow introduction, next a moderately fast section, then a *scherzo,* and lastly a broad, monumental finale, "While preserving in broad outline the four-movement convention [wrote Gray] the work viewed as a whole reveals the presence of the formal principle exemplified in orthodox sonata form—the triune symmetry of exposition, development, and recapitulation. In the slow introduction the chief protagonists make their appearance; in the following section they are worked out, in the *scherzo*-like episode fresh material is introduced, but development is still continued, and the final peroration is clearly in the nature of a recapitulation. The resultant form, therefore, is not merely one of four interlinked movements, but constitutes a single and indissoluble organism at the same time. In this respect the Seventh Symphony is from a purely abstract and objective point of view, unique."

As in the case of the first movement of the Fifth Symphony, there has been no lack of interpretations and many analysts have racked their brains over it, with very divergent results. Without going into the matter further or expressing an opinion on it, I should only like to mention that Ilmari Krohn found as a whole that it corresponds, not to a sonata—as Gray claims—but to a rondo composed of smaller elements, while Roiha subdivides the work into three sections, the first of which corresponds to the exposition of a sonata. The two others he defines as a "series of passage-like strophes" *(gang-artige Strophenserie).*

After the simple rising scale passage for strings in the introduction, with the syncopated, trailing double basses, we find a harmonic background for the first subject carried by the flutes:

EXAMPLE 65

Several expressive smaller motifs in the strings and wood-winds complete the picture, followed by the broad, sustained passage for strings that corresponds with the second subject of the exposition.

EXAMPLE 66

The great tension in the warm, intensive register, of which this is the beginning, ends in the powerful entry of the solo trombone, which introduces the closing group:

EXAMPLE 67

The section that, in Gray's opinion, corresponds to the beginning of a development and at the same time to a second movement, begins with the recurrence of the rising scale passage of the opening bars of the work, which is immediately followed by the modified first subject. The tempo quickens to a certain agitation, and the development continues with the same material in a dramatically intensified, rapidly accelerated transition to the *vivacissimo* that then in turn leads to a restatement of the powerful trombone theme in the minor over a foaming background in the strings. However, the dark mood lightens in a transition passage, which leads into the *scherzo* section. Here we also find a new series of motifs, which in the following progress of the movement are varied, developed and juxtaposed to form an enchanting harmonic texture. After one of Sibelius' typically long string passages, the big trombone theme is restated in the closing section against a figured background developed from the previous motifs. Several very varied repetitions of the motifs introduced in the exposition, first in a powerful crescendo and then in a subdued atmosphere in which the harmonies are reminiscent of the *Valse triste* (though quite unintentionally so, according to the Master) lead to the clear and definite closing bars of the work.

The great interest aroused by Sibelius in the United States led to his being commissioned by the New York Philharmonic Society to write a new orchestral work to be performed for the first time by this orchestra. This composition, which was entitled *Tapiola,* had its world *première* on December 26, 1925, in New York under the direction of Walter Damrosch. It was not played in Finland until two years later.

The name might lead one to believe that here we have to do with a pure Kalevala motif. In one way it can be so viewed, in others, not. The cantos of the Kalevala sing of no event that could be taken as a basis, though the name refers to Tapio, the forest god of Finnish mythology. "Tapiola" is the abode of the god Tapio and the score contains, as motto, a quatrain in German, French, and English, which according to the Master, he himself wrote at the request of his publisher. (The original Finnish text has not survived.)

> Widespread they stand, the Northland's dusky forests,
> Ancient, mysterious, brooding savage dreams;
> Within them dwells the Forest's mighty god,
> And woodsprites in the gloom weave magic secrets.

The symphonic poem begins with a string passage which consists of two bars of a few notes, moving in con-

EXAMPLE 68

junct motion within the compass of a fourth, each interval being limited to a second. This simple, fragmentary, and straightforward theme is so pregnant with possibilities that it was sufficient in the Master's hand to
form the germ cell of the entire work, which takes about
eighteen minutes to perform. At the very outset it is
repeated more than twenty times with trivial variations
by different instrumental combinations and the transformations it undergoes are infinite, in number and
extent. Even themes which at a hasty glance seem to
contain new material, are found on closer inspection
to be only variants or developments of the original idea.

The transformations of the melody show us (in the
words of Ernest Newman) "aspect after aspect of what
might be called the soul of the forest." And he closes by
saying, "as the forest is self-contained and self-complete,
so is the germ-theme of *Tapiola;* it assumes a score of
aspects while always retaining its original character."

The flowing, imaginative, bewitching texture resolves in a rising *crescendo* passage for the strings, extend-
ing over forty bars, which attains to an overpowering
pitch of intensity and culminates in a terrific outburst
from the whole orchestra. A couple of surging passages in
the woodwinds and strings lead to the work's wonderfully
beautiful epilogue. The string orchestra once more sings
a broad, intensive variant of the basic theme, counter-
pointed by lamenting woodwind voices. Slowly and with
passionate beauty it moves onward to a harmonic close
which is reached in the rich, satisfactory plagal cadence.
"The scoring is wonderful [wrote Elmer Diktonius of
the Seventh Symphony and *Tapiola*], neither sophisticated nor brilliant, but really splendid, throwing light
and shade over the whole like sunshine in a forest. Light,

rhythmically spiced string passages alternate with monotonous rumbles of the woodwinds—altogether, gaiety and moody meditation and a throbbing intensity that scarcely indicates senescent slackness in our glorious Master."

VIII

Negotium cum dignitate

S*ibelius' music* has now penetrated the consciousness of the world at large and has earned a recognition that comes to few living artists. This is not the place to render an account of the various honors and marks of esteem conferred upon him from far and near during past decades. The Master's work and endeavors and the results he has achieved will principally engage our attention.

In 1926 he completed the intense incidental music for Shakespeare's *Tempest,* ordered by the Royal Theatre of Copenhagen—a work that makes a fascinating impression, even as an independent concert suite. In addition, the list of compositions for that year also includes a couple of cantatas, and for the following year several smaller works, mostly for violin and piano.

Op. 116 is dated 1929, and since that time Sibelius has published nothing more. Up to now he has maintained his reticence regarding his work during the last two decades. "That's a sealed book," he replies imperturbably whenever one ventures to ask him about it; and then he adds—"For all that, foreign journalists nevertheless concoct all sorts of things."

But one thing is certain—judging by the intellectual youthfulness and buoyancy, the incredible mental alertness and vitality that still radiate from his whole person, and the physical health that he enjoys—one can no doubt be sure that he has not rested idly on his laurels. Probably the words that he spoke to Ekman in 1935 still hold good:

"My work has the same fascination for me now as when I was young, a fascination bound up with the difficulty of the task. Let no one imagine that composing is easier for an old composer, in so far as he takes his art seriously. The demands one makes on oneself increase with the passing years. Greater sureness makes one scorn more than formerly solutions that come too easily, that follow the line of least resistance. New problems are continually cropping up. The thing that has pleased me most is that I have been able to reject so much. The greatest labor I have expended, perhaps, was on works that have never been completed."

In a brief, final summing up it is natural to try to see Sibelius against the background of contemporary trends and to ascertain to what extent the Master's work has influenced modern composition.

To begin with, we may proceed from the point of view of the Danish critic, Hauch, more than thirty years ago, to which reference was made in the opening chapter of this work and which to all appearances is as true today as it was then. Fifteen years ago Frosterus described Sibelius' absolutely unique position in contemporary music in the following, equally appropriate terms: "He never aimed at being radically modern and cannot, in this sense, ever go out of date. His series of symphonies spring from the intense experiences of his youth, forming an airy span that links one golden age to another—the future. High above our crumbling civilization, entangled in doubts and hatred, rises his rainbow arch of tones."

But Frosterus is guilty of a great exaggeration when he asserts that from the "technical aspect Sibelius belongs to a past epoch." An analytical study of the tonal and rhythmical elements in his work and his treatment of the instruments furnishes altogether different information. Sibelius has learned and assimilated much from the technique of the old masters, but he has also derived just as much from modern technical achievements and the wider possibilities of expression that resulted from the shaking off of old traditions and beliefs, a development in which he himself has played a very great and active role.

On principle, Sibelius' attitude even today is wholly unbiased. For him there is no other norm than that which, with the unfailing instinct and vigilant fastidiousness of genius he imposes on himself. In this sense, Sibelius—though probably quite unintentionally—is not only radically modern but far in advance of his time, and in advance of its continued propensity—even in music's most radical manifestations—to dogmatize and standardize its technique.

From this point of view, Sibelius' influence on contemporary music is very insignificant. All the greater, we may assume, will be his influence in the future. On the other hand, it is not at all difficult to show that he has exercised a very pronounced influence on the style of contemporary music. Apart from Finland, where he seems to hold, involuntarily but irrevocably, a large number of young composers in the magic circle of his "Finnish" style and individualistic idiom, one also finds his characteristic style in much of the new music in both the old and the new worlds. Such influences can be very justly characterized as negative and more in line, from an artistic point of view, with the *Epigonentum* that dominated Germany after Richard Wagner.

Now we ask ourselves: has Sibelius exerted no really positive and fructifying influence on the music of his epoch? We are forced to admit that it really looks that way. His art is too ruthlessly personal, too weakly anchored in the stylistic consciousness of the age to find many adherents.

A Haydn and a Mozart wrote music in the classical style of their period, and they did it with sovereign mastery, administering their heritage and widening their domain in an admirable way; but they never departed from the Apollonian atmosphere of that "universal" (i. e., non-personal) equilibrium and harmony peculiar to their century. Beethoven also followed the same path. And yet he already stood on the threshold of a new age. Like them he was born at the right time. He stretched the conventional forms to the breaking point. His works were so strongly permeated with his individuality that it created both their style and atmosphere. Later this type of art developed into a much too human-personal matter for it to claim many adherents. True, Brahms looked upon it as stylistically authoritative, but he still had enough creative force of his own to compose in this spirit while retaining his own individuality. But then? With and after Wagner began the schools of the *epigoni* and everything of importance and value that has occurred in the world of music since that time, has been (as always, but here exclusively so) a product of independent minds and great personalities who have drawn their models from the past (positive and negative), have looked forward to the future, and have created something new according to the law of their own nature.

Among these, Jean Sibelius stands in the front ranks. For him, school and contemporary style have never consciously played a role. And that, I believe, is the essential criterion that he belongs both to the present and the future.

Complete List of Works

ORCHESTRAL WORKS

Opus No.	Title	Date
None	Overture in A minor	1890–91
None	Overture in E Major	1890–91
None	Scène de ballet	1891
9	En Saga	1892; rev. 1901
10	Overture, Karelia	1893
11	Suite, Karelia	1893
22, No. 3	Legend, The Swan of Tuonela	1893; rev. 1896 and 1900
16	Vårsång (Spring Song)	1894
None	Skogsrået (The Dryad)	1894
6	Cassation for small orchestra	1895
22, Nos. 1, 3, and 4	Legends: Lemminkäinen and the Maidens / Lemminkäinen in Tuonela / The Return of Lemminkäinen	1895; rev. 1896, No. 4 again rev. 1900, Nos. 1 and 3 rev. again 1939
39	Symphony No. 1 in E minor	1899
25	Scènes historiques I	1899; No. 3 rev. 1911
	1. All 'Overtura	
	2. Scène	
	3. Festivo	
26	Tone poem, Finlandia	1899; rev. 1900
43	Symphony No. 2 in D Major	1901
None	Cortège	1901

49	Symphonic fantasia, *Pohjola's Daughter*	1906
53	Dance intermezzo, *Pan and Echo*	1906; rev. 1909
52	Symphony No. 3 in C Major	1907
55	*Night Ride and Sunrise*	1909
59	Funeral march, *In Memoriam*	1909
45	Two pieces for orchestra	1910
	1. *The Dryads*	
	2. *Dance Intermezzo*	
62b	*Valse romantique,* for small orchestra	1911
63	Symphony No. 4 in A minor	1911
66	*Scènes historiques* II	1912
	1. *The Chase* (Overture)	
	2. *Love-song*	
	3. *At the Draw-bridge*	
64	Tone poem, *The Bard*	1913
73	Tone poem, *The Oceanides*	1914
82	Symphony No. 5 in E flat Major	1915; rev. 1916; largely rewritten 1919
87a	Impromptu	1917
96	Three pieces for orchestra	1920
	1. *Valse lyrique*	
	2. *Autrefois, scène pastorale*[1]	
	3. *Valse chevaleresque*	
100	*Scène caractéristique*	1922
104	Symphony No. 6 in D minor	1923
105	Symphony No. 7 in C Major	1924
112	Symphonic poem, *Tapiola*	1925
None	*Tempo di minuetto* (Listed by Gray)	?
None	Academic March (Listed by Gerald Abraham)	?

[1] This has also been arranged as a duet.

WORKS FOR SOLO INSTRUMENT WITH ORCHESTRA

47	Concerto in D minor for violin and orchestra	1903; rev. 1905
69	Two Serenades for violin and orchestra	
	No. 1 in D Major	1912
	No. 2 in G minor	1913
77	Two Pieces for violin or cello and small orchestra	
	1. *Cantique (Laetare anima mea)*	1914
	2. *Devotion (Ab imo pectore)*	1915
87b	Two Humoresques for violin and orchestra	1917
	No. 1 in D minor	
	No. 2 in D Major	
89	Four Humoresques for violin and orchestra	1917
	No. 1 in G minor;	
	No. 2 in G minor;	
	No. 3 in E flat Major;	
	No. 4 in G minor	

WORKS FOR STRING ORCHESTRA

None	*Porträtterna (Portraits)*	1901
42	Romance in C Major	1903
14	*Rakastava (The Lover)*[2]	1911
	1. *The Lover*	
	2. *The Path of the Beloved*	
	3. *Good Night—Farewell*	
62a	*Canzonetta*	1911
98a	*Suite mignonne,* for two flutes and strings	1921
98b	*Suite champêtre*	1921

[2] Based on a work for male voices (Kanteletar, 1895).

| None | *Andante festivo* | 1924 |
| None | *Andante lirico* | 1924 |

WORKS FOR BRASS BAND

| None | *Tiera* | 1894 |

CHAMBER MUSIC

None	Trio in A minor	1881–82
None	Piano quartet in E minor	1881–82
None	Sonata for violin and piano	1883
None	Andantino for cello and piano	1884
None	String quartet in E flat Major	1885
None	Sonata in F Major for violin and piano	1886
None	Piano Trio	1887
None	Theme and Variations in C sharp minor for string quartet	1888
2	Two pieces (Romance and Epilogue) for violin and piano	1888; rev. 1912
None	Suite in A Major for violin, viola, and cello	1889
None	String quartet in A minor	1889
4	String quartet in B flat Major	1889
None	Piano quintet in G minor	1889
None	Piano quartet in C Major	1891
None	Octet for flute, clarinet, and strings (material afterwards used in *En Saga*)	1891
None	Rondo for viola and piano	1895
20	*Malinconia,* for cello and piano	1901
56	String quartet in D minor (*Voces intimae*)	1909
78	Four pieces for violin (or cello) and piano	1915
79	Six pieces for violin and piano	1915

List of Works

80	Sonatina in E Major for violin and piano	1915
81	Five pieces for violin and piano	1915
102	*Novelette,* for violin and piano	1923
106	*Danses champêtres,* five pieces for violin and piano	1925
115	Four pieces for violin and piano	1929

ORGAN MUSIC

111	Two pieces	
	1. *Intrada*	1926
	2. *Sorgmusik* (Funeral)	1931

PIANO MUSIC

24	Ten pieces	
	1. *Impromptu*	1894
	2. *Romance in A flat Major*	1894
	3. *Caprice*	1895
	4. *Romance*	1895
	5. *Waltz*	1895
	6. *Idyll*	1895
	7. *Andantino*	1895
	8. *Nocturne*	1900
	9. *Romance in D flat Major*	1903
	10. *Barcarolle*	1903
None	*The Cavalier*	1901
None	Six Finnish folk songs	1903
41	*Kyllikki,* three lyric pieces	1904
58	Ten pieces	1909
	1. *Rêverie*	
	2. *Scherzino*	
	3. *Air varié*	
	4. *The Shepherd*	
	5. *The Evening*	
	6. *Dialogue*	
	7. *Tempo di menuetto*	

167

	8. *Fisher Song*	
	9. *Serenade*	
	10. *Summer Song*	
67	Three Sonatinas	1912
	1. *F sharp minor*	
	2. *E Major*	
	3. *B flat minor*	
68	Two Rondinos	1912
	1. *G sharp minor*	
	2. *C sharp minor*	
40	*Pensées lyriques*	1912–14
	1. *Valsette*	
	2. *Chant sans paroles*	
	3. *Humoresque*	
	4. *Menuetto*	
	5. *Berceuse*	
	6. *Pensée mélodique*	
	7. *Rondoletto*	
	8. *Scherzando* ⎫	
	9. *Petite Sérénade* ⎬ added later	
	10. *Polonaise* ⎭	
None	*Spagnuolo*	1913
74	Four lyric pieces	1914
	1. *Eclogue*	
	2. *Soft west Wind*	
	3. *At the Dance*	
	4. *In the old Home*	
75	Five Pieces	1914
	1. *When the Mountain-ash is in Flower*	
	2. *The solitary Tree*	
	3. *The Aspen*	
	4. *The Birch Tree*	
	5. *The Fir Tree*	
76	Thirteen Pieces	1914
	1. *Esquisse*	

2. *Staccato*
3. *Carillon*
4. *Humoresque*
5. *Consolation*
6. *Romanzetta*
7. *Affettuoso*
8. *Pièce enfantine*
9. *Arabesque (Musical Box)*
10. *Elegiaco*
11. *The twin Flowers of the North* (Linnea)
12. *Capricietto*
13. *Harlequinade*

34 Bagatelles   1914–16
1. *Waltz*
2. *Dance Air*
3. *Mazurka*
4. *Humorous*
5. *Drollery*
6. *Rêverie*
7. *Pastoral Dance*
8. *The Harper*
9. *Reconnaissance* ⎫
10. *Souvenir*   ⎬ added later

85 Five Pieces   1916
1. *Bluebells*
2. *The Carnation*
3. *The Iris*
4. *The Snapdragon*
5. *The Campanula*

None *Mandolinata*   1917
94 Six pieces   1919
1. *Dance*
2. *Novelette*
3. *Sonnet*
4. *Berger et Bergerette*

	5. *Mélodie*	
	6. *Gavotte*	
97	Six Bagatelles	1920
	1. *Humoresque*	
	2. *Song*	
	3. *Little Waltz*	
	4. *Humorous March*	
	5. *Impromptu*	
	6. *Humoresque*	
None	*Pièce romantique*	1920
None	*Till trånaden* (Longing)	1920
99	Eight short pieces	1922
	1. *Pièce humoristique*	
	2. *Esquisse*	
	3. *Souvenir*	
	4. *Impromptu*	
	5. *Couplet*	
	6. *Animoso*	
	7. *Moment de valse*	
	8. *Petite marche*	
101	Five romantic pieces	1923
	1. *Romance*	
	2. *Chant du soir*	
	3. *Scène lyrique*	
	4. *Humoresque*	
	5. *Scène romantique*	
103	Five characteristic impressions	1924
	1. *The Village Church*	
	2. *The Fiddler*	
	3. *The Oarsman*	
	4. *The Storm*	
	5. *In Mournful Mood*	
114	*Esquisses*	1929
	1. *Landscape*	
	2. *Winter Scene*	
	3. *Forest Lake*	

4. *Song in the Forest*
5. *Spring Vision*

5	Six Impromptus for pianoforte	?
12	Sonata in F Major	1893

OPERAS

None	*Weneen Luominen (The Creation of the Boat)* (sketches only)	1893
None	*The Maiden in the Tower,* in one act	1896

INCIDENTAL MUSIC

None	Two songs with piano trio for Wennerberg's *Necken (The Watersprite)*	1888
27	To Adolf Paul's *King Christian II*	1898

  1. a. *Élégie*
    b. *Musette*
    c. *Minuet*
    d. *Fool's Song of the Spider*
  2. a. *Nocturne*
    b. *Serenade*
  3. Ballad

44	To Järnefelt's *Kuolema (Death)*	1903

  1. *Introduction*
  2. *Scene with Cranes*
  3. *Valse triste*

46	To Maeterlinck's Pelléas et Mélisande	1905

  1. *At the Castle Gate*
  2. *Mélisande*
  3. *On the Sea-shore*
  4. *A Spring in the Park*
  5. *The three blind Sisters*[3]

[3] Also arranged for solo voice with orchestra or piano.

6. *Pastorale*
7. *Mélisande at the Spinning-wheel*
8. *Entr'acte*
9. *The Death of Mélisande*

51   To Hjalmar Procopé's *Belshazar gästabud (Belshazzar's Feast)*   1906
1. *Oriental Procession*
2. *Solitude*
3. *Night Music*
4. *Khadra's Dance*

54   To August Strindberg's *Swanwhite*   1908
1. *The Peacock*
2. *The Harp*
3. *The Maiden with the Roses*
4. *Listen, the Robin sings*
5. *The Prince Alone*
6. *Swanwhite and the Prince*
7. *Song of Praise*

8   To Mikael Lybeck's *Odlan (The Lizard)*   1909

None   To Adolf Paul's *The Language of the Birds*   1911

71   To Poul Knudsen's pantomime *Scaramouche*   1913

83   To Hugo von Hofmannsthal's *Everyman*   1916

109   To Shakespeare's *The Tempest*   1926
a. Prelude
b. Suite I
  1. *The Oak Tree*
  2. *Humoreske*
  3. *Caliban's Song*

    4. *The Harvesters*
    5. *Canon*
    6. *Scène*
    7. *Berceuse*
    8. *Entr'acte*
    9. *The Storm*
  c. Suite II
    1. *Chorus of Winds*
    2. *Intermezzo*
    3. *Dance of the Nymphs*
    4. *Prospero*
    5. *Songs 1 and 2*
    6. *Miranda*
    7. *The Naiads*
    8. *Dance Episode*

CANTATAS AND CHORAL MUSIC

7	*Kullervo* (from the Kalevala), symphony for soli, chorus, and orchestra	1892
18	Six part-songs for male voices *a cappella*	
	1. *Sortunut ääni (The Broken Voice)* (Kanteletar)	1899
	2. *Terve kuu (Hail Moon)* (Kalevala)	1901
	3. *Venematka (The Boat Journey)* (Kalevala)	1893
	4. *Saarella palaa (Fire on the Island)* (Kanteletar)	1895
	5. *Metsämiehen laulu (The Woodman's Song) (Kivi)*	1895
	6. *Sydämeni laulu (The Song of my Heart (Kivi)*	1895
None	*Rakastava (The Lover)* (Kanteletar), for male voices	

	a cappella (afterwards used in the suite for strings, Op. 14)	1895
None	*University Cantata for the Year 1894* (Leino), for chorus and orchestra	1894
None	*Mis rastas raataa (Busy as a Thrush)* (Kanteletar), for male chorus *a cappella*	1894
None	*Cantata for the Coronation of Nicholas II* (Cajander), for soli, chorus, and orchestra	1895
None	*Päiv'ei pääse (The Day not ended)* (Erkko), for children's voices *a cappella*	1896
23	*University Cantata for the Year 1897* (Forsman), for mixed chorus *a cappella* (only parts for mixed chorus *a cappella* have been published)	1897
28	*Sandels* (Runeberg), improvisation for male chorus and orchestra	1898
None	*Yks'voima (One Power)* (Cajander), for male chorus *a cappella*	1898
21	*Natus in Curas,* hymn for male chorus *a cappella*	(publ. 1899)
31, No. 3	*Atenarnes sång (Song of the Athenians)* (Rydberg), for boys' and men's voices, saxhorn septet, triangle, bass drum, and cymbals (alternative accompaniment for wind band)	1899
32	*Tulen synty (The Origin of Fire)* (Kalevala), for baritone solo, male chorus, and orchestra	1902

19	*Impromptu (Thou who guidest the Stars)* (Rydberg), for four-part women's chorus and orchestra	1902, rev. 1910
None	*Ej med klagan (Not with Lamentation)* (Runeberg), for mixed chorus *a cappella*	1905
None	*Koulutie (The Way to School)* (Koskenniemi), for children's voices *a cappella*	1913
None	*Three Songs for American Schools* (English words), for children's voices *a cappella*	1913
84	Five part-songs for male chorus *a capella*	1915

    1. *Herr Lager* (Fröding)
    2. *På berget (On the Mountain)* (Fröding)
    3. *Ett drömackord (A Dream Chord)* (Fröding)
    4. *Evige Eros (Eternal Eros)* (Fröding)
    5. *Till havs (At Sea)* (Reuter)

None	*Fridolins dårskap (Fridolin's Folly)* (Karlfeldt), for male chorus *a cappella*	1917
91	a. *March of the Finnish Light Infantry* (Nurmio), for male voices and orchestra	1917
	b. *Scout March,* for orchestra and four-part chorus *(ad. lib.)*	1918
None	Two songs (G. Schybergson) for male chorus *a cappella*	1918

    1. *Ute hörs stormen*
    2. *Brusande rusar en våg*

92	*Oma maa (Our Native Land)* (Kallio), cantata for chorus and orchestra	1918
93	*Jordens sång (Song of the Earth)* (Jarl Hemmer), cantata for chorus and orchestra, for the inauguration of Turku University	1919
95	*Maan virsi (Hymn of the Earth)* (Eino Leino), cantata for chorus and orchestra	1920
None	*Jone havsfärd (Jonah's Voyage)* (Fröding), for male chorus *a cappella*	1920
None	*Veljeni (Brotherhood)* (Aho), for male chorus *a cappella*	1920
None	*Likhet (Resemblance)* (Runeberg), for male chorus *a cappella*	1920
None	*Viipurin Laulu-Veikkojen (V.S. Bin) kunniamarssi (I) (Honor March (I) of the singing Brothers of Viborg)* (E. Eerola)	1921
107	*Hymn,* for chorus and organ	1925
108	Two part-songs (Larin Kyösti) for male chorus *a cappella*	1925
	1. *Humoreski* (Kyösti)	
	2. *Ne pitkän* (Kyösti)	
None	Two psalms for mixed chorus *a cappella*	1925–27
110	*Väinön virsi (The Hymn of Väinö)* (Kalevala), for chorus and orchestra	1926
113	*Masonic Ritual Music,* for male voices and piano or organ (the whole suite revised in 1948)	

1.	*Introduction*	1927
2.	*Thoughts be our Comfort* (Schiller)	1927
3.	*Introduction and Hymn* (Confucius)	1927
4.	*Marcia* (Goethe)	1927
5.	*Light* (J. A. Simelius)	1927
6.	*Salem (Onward, Ye Brethren)* (Rydberg)[4]	1927
7.	*Whosoever hath a Love* (Rydberg)	1927
8.	*Ode to Fraternity* (S. Sario)	1946
9.	*Hymn* (S. Sario)	1946
10.	*Marche funèbre*	1927
11.	*Ode* (S. Korpela)	1927
12.	*Finlandia Hymn* (V. Sola)[5]	1938

None	*Siltavahti (The Guard of the Bridge)* (V. Sola), for male chorus *a cappella* (Honor march of the chorus New Yorkin Laulu-Miehet)[6]	1929
None	*Viipurin Lauluveikkojen kunniamarssi (II) (Honor march (II) of the singing Brothers of Viborg)* (E. Eerola), for male chorus *a cappella*	1929
None	*Karjalan osa (Karelia's Fate)* (R. Nurminen), for male voices and piano	(publ. 1930)
31, No. 1	*Laulu Lemminkäiselle (Song for Lemminkäinen)* (Y. Veijola)	Date unknown
48	*The Captive Queen,* ballad for chorus and orchestra	1906

[4] Published in several arrangements under the title "Onward, Ye Brethren!"

[5] Arranged by the composer from *Finlandia,* Op. 26.

[6] Also arranged for solo voice and piano by the composer.

65	Two part-songs for mixed chorus *a cappella:* (a) *People of Land and Sea* (1912); (b) *Bell Melody of Berghäll Church* (1912)	

WORKS FOR SOLO VOICE AND ORCHESTRA

3	Arioso *(Flickans årstider) (The Maiden's Seasons)* (Runeberg), for voice and string orchestra	1893; rev. 1911
33	*Koskenlaskijan morsiamet (The Ferryman's Brides)* (Oksanen), for baritone, or mezzosoprano, and orchestra	1897
27, No. 1	d. *Sången om korsspindeln (Fool's Song of the Spider)* (from Paul's play *King Christian II,* for voice and orchestra or piano)	1898
38, No. 1	*Höstkväll (Autumn Night)* (Rydberg), for soprano, or tenor, and orchestra (or piano)	1904
46, No. 5	*Les trois soeurs aveugles (The three blind Sisters)* (from Maeterlinck's play *Pelléas et Mélisande)*[7]	1905
51, No. 5	*Den judiska flickan säng* (Song of the Jewess) (from Procopé's play *Belshazzar's Feast)*	1906
70	*Luonnotar* (Kalevala), tone poem for soprano and orchestra	1913

SONGS (WITH PIANO)[8]

None	Serenade (Runeberg)	1888

[7] Also for orchestra.

[8] Many of the songs have also been orchestrated by different Finnish composers.

13   Seven songs of Runeberg
       1. *Under strandens granar*
          ('Neath the Fir-trees)   1892
       2. *Kyssens hopp (A Kiss's*
          Hope)   1892
       3. *Hjärtats morgon (The*
          Heart's Morning)   1891
       4. *Våren flyktar hastigt*
          (Spring is flying)   1891
       5. *Drömmen (The Dream)*   1891
       6. *Till Frigga (To Frigga)*   1892
       7. Järgargossen *(The young*
          Sportsman)   1891
1   *Julvisor (Five Christmas Songs)*   1895
17   Seven songs
       1. *Sen har jag ej frågat mera*
          (And I questioned then
          no further) (Runeberg)   1899
       2. *Sov in! (Slumber)*
          (Tavaststjerna)   1894
       3. *Fågellek (Enticement)*
          (Tavaststjerna)   1894
       4. *Vilse (Astray)*
          (Tavaststjerna)   1894
       5. *En slända (The Dragon-*
          fly) (Lavertin)   1894
       6. *Illalle (To Evening)*
          (Forsman)   1898
       7. *Lastu lainehilla (Drift-*
          wood) (Calamnius)   1898
None   Segelfahrt (Sailing) (Ohqvist)   1899
36   Six songs   1899
       1. *Svarta rosor (Black Roses)*
          (Josephson)
       2. *Men min fågel märks dock*
          icke (But my bird is long

in homing) (Runeberg)
3. *Bollspelet vid Trianon
(Tennis at Trianon)*
(Fröding)
4. *Säv säv susa (Sigh Sedges
Sigh)* (Fröding)
5. *Marssnön (March Snow)*
(Wecksell)
6. *Demanten på marssnön
(The Diamond)*[9]
(Wecksell)

None	*Hymn till Thaïs (Hymn to Thaïs)* (A. Borgström)	1900
37	Five songs	
	1. *Den första kyssen (The first Kiss)* (Runeberg)	1898
	2. *Lasse liten (Berceuse)* (Topelius)	1902
	3. *Solluppgång (Sunrise)* (Hedberg)	1902
	4. *Var det en dröm? (Was it a Dream?)* (Wecksell)	1902
	5. *Flickan kom från sin älsklings möte (The Tryst)* (Runeberg)	1901
38	Five songs	1904

1. *Höstkväll (Autumn
Night)* (Rydberg)[10]
2. *På verandan vid havet
(On a Balcony by the Sea)*
(Rydberg)
3. *I natten (Night)* (Rydberg)
4. *Harpolekaren och hans
son (The Harper and his*

[9] There is also an original version with orchestral accompaniment.
[10] Also with original orchestral accompaniment.

Son) (Rydberg)

5. *Jag ville jag vore (I would I were dwelling)* (Fröding)

50   Six songs   1906
1. *Lenzgesang (A Song of Spring)* (Fitger)
2. *Sehnsucht (Longing)* (Weiss)
3. *Im Feld ein Mädchen singt (A Maiden yonder sings)* (Susman)
4. *Aus banger Brust (O wert thou here)* (Dehmel)
5. *Die stille Stadt (The silent Town)* (Dehmel)
6. *Rosenlied (The Song of the Roses)* (Ritter)

35   Two songs   1907
1. *Jubal* (Josephson)
2. *Theodora* (Gripenberg)

57   Eight songs of Josephson   1909
1. *Alvan och snigeln (The Snail)*
2. *En blomma stod vid vägen (The wild Flower)*
3. *Kvarnhjulet (The Millwheel)*
4. *Maj (May)*
5. *Jag är ett träd (The Tree)*
6. *Hertig Magnus (Baron Magnus)*
7. *Väskapens blomma (Friendship)*
8. *Näcken (The Elf-king)*

60   Two songs from Shakespeare's

Twelfth Night
(anonymous Swedish
translation)   1909
  1. *Come away, Death*
  2. *When that I was and a
    little tiny boy*

61   Eight songs   1910
  1. *Långsamt som kvällskyn
    (Slow as the Colors)*
    (Tavaststjerna)
  2. *Vattenplask (Lapping
    Waters)* (Rydberg)
  3. *När jag drömmer (When
    I dream)* (Tavaststjerna)
  4. *Romeo* (Tavaststjerna)
  5. *Romance* (Tavaststjerna)
  6. *Dolce far niente*
    (Tavaststjerna)
  7. *Fåfäng önskan (Idle
    Wishes)* (Runeberg)
  8. *Vårtagen (The Spell of
    Springtide)* (Gripenberg)

72   Six songs
  1. *Vi ses igen (Farewell)*
    (Rydberg)   1914
  2. *Orions bälte (Orion's
    Girdle)* (Topelius)   1914
  3. *Kyssen (The Kiss)*
    (Rydberg)   1915
  4. *Kaiutar (The Echo
    Nymph)* (Larin Kyösti)   1915
  5. *Der Wanderer und der
    Bach (The Wanderer and
    the Brook)* (Greif)   1915
  6. *Hundra vägar (A Hun-
    dred Ways)* (Runeberg)   1915

86   Six songs (Swedish text only)   1916
          1. *Vårförnimmelser (The
             Coming of Spring)*
             (Tavaststjerna)
          2. *Längtan heter min arvedel
             (Longing is my Heritage)*
             (Karlfeldt)
          3. *Dold förening (Hidden
             Union)* (Snoilsky)
          4. *Och finns det en tanke
             (And is there a Thought?)*
             (Tavaststjerna)
          5. *Sångarlön (The Singer's
             Reward)* (Snoilsky)
          6. *I systrar, I bröder (Ye Sis-
             ters and Brothers)* (Lybeck)

88   Six songs   1917
          1. *Blåsippan (The blue
             Anemone)* (Franzén)
          2. *De bägge rosorna (The
             two Roses)* (Franzén)
          3. *Vitsippan (The Star-
             flower)* (Franzén)
          4. *Sippan (The Anemone)*
             (Runeberg)
          5. *Törnet (The Thornbush)*
             (Runeberg)
          6. *Blommans öde (The
             Flower)* (Runeberg)

90   Six songs (Runeberg)   1917
          1. *Norden (The North)*
          2. *Hennes budskap (Her
             Message)*
          3. *Morgonen (The Morning)*
          4. *Fågelfängaren
             (The Bird-catcher)*

5. *Sommarnatten*
(Summer Night)

6. *Vem styrde hit din väg?*
(Who has brought
you here?)

None	*Narciss* (Gripenberg)	1918
None	*Små flickor (Little Girls)*	
	(Procopé)	1918
None	*Erloschen (Extinct)*	
	(Busse-Palmo)	1918
None	*Sinisorsa (The blue Duck)*	
	(Koskimies)	(publ. 1925)

VOCAL DUETS

None	*Tanken (The Thought)*	
	(Runeberg), for two sopranos	
	and piano	1915
96b	*Autrefois, scène pastorale* (Hj.	
	Procopé), for soprano, mezzo-	
	soprano, and orchestra[11]	1920

MELODRAMAS

None	*Trånaden (Longing)*	
	(E. J. Stagnelius), for	
	recitation and piano	1887
None	*Svartsjukans nätter (Nights of*	
	Jealousy) (Runeberg), for	
	recitation and piano trio	1888
15	*Skogsrået (The Dryad)*	
	(Rydberg), for recitation and	
	piano, two horns, and	
	string orchestra	1894
30	*Islossningen i Ule älv (The*	
	Breaking of the Ice on Ule	

[11] Also arranged for orchestra.

	River) (Topelius), for recitation, male chorus, and orchestra	1899
29	*Snöfrid* (Rydberg), for recitation, chorus, and orchestra	1900
None	*Ett ensamt skidspår (The lonely Ski Trail)* (Gripenberg), for recitation and piano[12]	1925

[12] Orchestrated by composer in 1948.

Bibliography*

Abraham, Gerald, (ed.). *Sibelius, a Symposium*. London, 1947.

Diktonius, Elmer. *Opus 12, Musik*. Helsinki, 1933.

Downes, Olin. *Symphonic Broadcasts*. New York, 1932.

Ekman, Karl. *Jean Sibelius*. (Helsinki, 1935. English translation by Edward Birse, with foreword by Ernest Newman.

Flodin, Karl. *Finska musiker*. Helsinki, 1900.

Frosterus, Sigurd. *Stålåderns janusansikte*. Helsinki, 1935.

Furuhjelm, Erik. *Jean Sibelius*. Borgå, 1916.

Gray, Cecil. *Jean Sibelius*. London, 1931.

———. *Sibelius: The Symphonies*. Oxford, 1935.

Hauch, Gunnar. *Jean Sibelius*. Tilskueren, 1914.

Järnefelt, Arvid. *Vanhempieni romaani II*. Helsinki, 1922.

Konow, Walter von. *Muistoja Jean Sibeliuksen polkavuosilta*. Helsinki, 1925.

Kotilainen, Otto. *Mestarin muokattavana*. Helsinki, 1925.

Krohn, Ilmari. *Der Formenbau in den Symphonien von Jean Sibelius*. Helsinki, 1942.

———. *Der Stimmungsgehalt der Symphonien von Jean Sibelius, I–II*. Helsinki, 1945–46.

Lambert, Constant. *Music Ho!* London, 1934.

Madetoja, Leevi. *Jean Sibelius oppetajana*. Helsinki, 1925.

Newmarch, Rosa. *Jean Sibelius*. Boston, 1939.

Niemann, Walter. *Jean Sibelius*. Leipzig, 1917.

* A complete bibliography accompanies the author's article on Sibelius in Sohlman's *Musiklexikon*, ed, Gösta Morin. (Sohlman's förlag, Stockholm, 1948–51), 270.

Ringbom, Nils-Eric. *Helsingfors orkesterföretag 1882–1932.* Helsinki, 1932.

Roiha, Eino. *Die Symphonien von Jean Sibelius.* Jyväskylä, 1941.

Tanzberger, Ernst. *Die symphonischen Dichtungen von Jean Sibelius.* Würzburg, 1943.

Törne, Bengt von. *Sibelius, a Close-up.* London, 1937.

Väisänen, A. O. *Sibelius ja kansanmusiikki* (Kalevalan vuosikirja No. 16). Helsinki, 1936.

Index

Åbo: 5 n.
Aalottaret: 126
A Book about a Man: 19
Abraham, Gerald: 164, 186
Academy of Music: 11, 14 ff., 20, 37, 54–55
a cappella choral works: 84
Ackte, Aino: 67
Aho, Juhani: 33, 132, 176
Aino: 21 n.
Ainola: 88, 122, 140
Aino Symphony: 21, 30
Aino tryptich: 33
Allgemeine Deutsche Musikverein: 68 f.
Amsterdam: 68
Archaisms: 58
Augusteo Orchestra: 145

Baden: 108
Bantock, Granville: 91, 99
Bassoon, employment of: 75
Bayreuth: 53
Becker, Albert: 19
Beethoven, Ludwig van: 18, 27, 97, 100, 146, 161
Bergen: 134
Berlin: 19 f., 27, 68, 70, 90 f., 99, 107 f., 122
Berlin Philharmonic Orchestra: 21, 85

Berlioz, Hector: 118, 120
Bern Convention: 133
Birmingham: 91
Bobrikow: 64
Borg, Maria Charlotta: 4
Borgström, A.: 180
Borodin, Alexander: 61
Boston Symphony Orchestra: 130
Brahms, Johannes: 20, 23, 161
Brahms-Wagner feud: 20, 23, 27
Breitkopf & Härtel: 44, 86, 133
Bruch, Max: 125
Bruckner, Anton: 23; B Major Symphony, 123
Brussels: 68
Bungert, August: 20
Busoni, Ferruccio: 14, 15, 23, 90, 144
Bussler, Ludwig: 12
Busse-Palmo: 184

Cajander: 174
Calamnius: 179
Chamber music: 8, 9
Childhood environment: 5, 6
Choral works, *a cappella:* 84
Civil war (Finland): 141
Collan, Karl: 29
Concerto, violin: 88
Confucius: 177
Copenhagen: 68, 133, 158

Index

Crawford, J. W.: 21n.
Crust Symphony: 108

Dactylic metre: 113
Damrosch, Walter: 155
Debussy, Claude: 99, 118 ff., 126 128
Dehmel, Richard: 181
Diktonius, Elmer: 41, 108, 120, 146, 156, 186
d'Indy, Vincent: 99
Don Juan: 21
Dorian mode: 147
Downes, Olin: 39, 186
Dvořák, Anton: 68, 125

East Nyland: 4
Eerola, E: 176
Ekman, Ida: 67, 134
Ekman, Karl: 4, 12, 16 n., 21, 65, 69, 90, 133, 142 ff., 159, 186
Elgar, Edward: 99
Employment of bassoon: 75
Environment, childhood: 5 f.
Epigonentum: 20
Erkko, J. H.: 44, 174
Ethnographic material: 80
Ethnography: 29

Faltin, Richard: 70
Festival, Heidelberg: 69
"Finis Finlandiae": 107
Finland, Declaration of Independence: 141
Finnish idiom: 37
Finnish monetary system: 32 n.
Finnish Musicians: 66
Finnish national traits: 147
Finnish postal system, Russification of: 32 n.
Finnish Rhapsodies: 30
Finnish style: 80
Fitger: 181

Flodin, Karl: 13, 14 f., 17, 26, 35 f., 51, 66, 71, 88 f., 186
Flute: 55
Folk-music motifs: 31
Forsman: 174, 179
Franzen: 183
Fröding: 175, 176, 180, 181
Frosterus, Sigurd: 39, 40, 43, 46, 66, 72, 106, 107, 118, 135, 140, 159, 160, 186
Fuchs, Robert: 23, 24
Furuhjelm, Erik: v, 8, 13, 16, 24, 26, 33, 35, 40, 43, 83, 115, 128, 186

Gallen, Axel: 21, 32, 33, 41, 56
Göteborg: 68, 107, 124, 134, 145
Goethe, Johann Wolfgang von: 177
Goldmark, Carl: 23 ff.
Gray, Cecil: re title of Spring Song, 43; analysis of First Symphony, 59 f.; myth of Pohjola's Daughter, 92 n., re Voces intimae, 100; appraisal of Fourth Symphony, 108, 114, 122, 136, 145; appraisal of Sixth Symphony, 147, 149 f., 152, 154, 164, 186
Greif: 182
Grieg, Edvard Hagerup: 9, 13, 92
Gripenberg: 181, 182, 184, 185

Haapanen, Toive: 138
Hämeenlinna: 5 n.
Halir, Karl: 90
Hamburg: 68
Hangö: 86
Hanslick, Eduard: 51, 52
Hardy, Thomas: cited, 108
Hauch, Gunnar: 3, 159, 186
Haydn, Joseph: 100, 161
Hedberg: 180
Heidelberg: 68 ff., 108
Hellenic Rondo: 143
Helsingfors: 5 n.

Helsinki: 5n., 9, 20, 22, 26, 29, 32, 35, 39, 41, 64, 67, 70, 87, 94, 97, 115, 129, 134, 140, 142, 145
Helsinki Municipal Orchestra: 134f.
Helsinki Musikförening: 15
Helsinki Philharmonic Orchestra: 15, 16n., 67
Hemmer, Jarl: 176
Hensen, Wilhelm: 133
Hiawatha: 21n.
Hoffmannsthal, Hugo von: 172
Hungarian Rhapsodies: 29

Iceland: 108
Idiom, Finnish: 37
Ilmarinen: 21n.
Ilmatar: 21n.
Impressionism: 117ff.
Independence, Declaration of (Finland): 141
Ingelius, Axel Gabriel: 29
Inscription, *Swan of Tuonela:* 46n.
Inspirations from Kalevala: 29

Järnefelt, Aino: 23, 37
Järnefelt, Armas: 32, 53, 67
Järnefelt, Arvid: 28, 32, 85, 171, 186
Järnefelt, August Alexander: 22
Järnefelt, Eero: 32; expedition to Koli, 115; Fourth Symphony dedicated to, 116
Järnefelt, Maikki: soloist, Paris Exposition, 67
Järvenpää: 87
Jalas, Jussi: 147, 148
Joachim Quartet: 20
Josephson: 179, 181
Juha: 132

Karelia: runic singers, 36; scene of

honeymoon, 37; ancient history of province, 42
Karlfeldt: 175, 183
Karlsruhe: 69
Kajanus, Robert: 15, 16, 21, 22, 26, 29; takes up idea of "national" Finnish music, 30; asks Sibelius to write "popular" work, 38; member of the Symposium, 41; takes orchestra to Paris Exposition, 67; Sibelius dedicates *Pohjola's Daughter* to him, 92; conducts festival concert, 134; persuades Sibelius to move to Helsinki, 142
Kalalahti: 10
Kalevala (corpus of Finnish mythology): 21, 91, 93, 118, 126, 155, 173, 174, 176; English translations of 21n.; as inspiration, 22, 29; Kajanus and Kalevala myths, 30; adventures of Kullervo, 34n.; runic songs, 37; opera on Kalevala motif, 44; Kalevala Legends, 45ff.; six-part songs to Kalevala texts, 85; ballet on Kalevala motifs, 132
Kalevala Legend: 14
Kallio: 176
Kanteletar: 165, 173, 174; lyrics, 82; six-part songs 85
Kervo: 70
Kirby, W. F.: 21n.
Kivi, Aleksis: 85
Knudsen, P.: 172
Koli: 115, 116
Kompositionslehre (Marx): 9
Konow, Walter von: reminiscences, 6f., 186
Korpela, S.: 176
Koskenniemi: 175
Koskimies: 184

Index

Kotilainen, Otto: reminiscences, 54f., 186
Krohn, Ilmari: analysis of Fifth Symphony, 152, 186
Kullervo: 21n., 58; Symphony, 33; death of, 34n.; appraisal of symphony, 35; Finnish style in, 80
Kullervo Funeral March (Kajanus): 30
Kullervo Overture (von Schantz): 30
Kuopio: 44
Kyllikki: 45

Lambert, Constant: 146, 186
Lamoureux Orchestra: 91
Lake Tuusula: 87
La Mer: 126
Lake Vanajavesi: 10
La Patrie: French title of Finlandia, 65
Lappviken Asylum: 142
L'Après-midi d'un faune: 126
La tristesse du printemps: 43
Lavertin: 179
Legge, Walter: 58
Leino, Eino: 174, 176
Leipzig: 107
Leitmotifs: interpretation by, 144
Leitmotif technique: 48; Sibelius' attitude to, 58
Lemminkäinen: 21n., 46
Lessmann, Otto: 68f.
Levander, Gustav: 6
Libau: 107
Liverpool: 90
Liszt, Franz: 29
Living pictures: music for, 65
Lönrot, Elias: 21n.
Lohengrin: 53
London: 91, 93, 132, 144
Louhi: 21n.
Lovisa: 4, 6, 10, 70

Lübeck: 68
Lybeck, Mikaël: 33, 172, 183

Maeterlinck, Maurice: 92, 119, 171, 178
Madetoja, Leevi: reminiscences, 54f.; on First Symphony, 60, 132, 186
Mahler, Gustav: 97
Malmö: 68
Manchester: 90
Manifest, Postal: 32n.
Marx, Adolf Bernhard: 9
Meistersinger: 20
Melodrama: 81
Mendelssohn, Felix: 12
Merikanto, Oskar: 67
Metre: dactylic, 113; trochaic, 121
Mielck, Ernst: 67
Mode, Dorian: 147
Modern Music Series: 90
Moscow: 94
Motifs, folk-music: 31
Mozart, Wolfgang Amadeus: 21, 161
Musical Society: 29
Music Ho!: cited, 146
Musical visions: 56
Musikverein, Allgemeine Deutsche: 68f.
Mussorgsky, Modest: 118, 120

"Nation": 19n.
National Finnish Movement: 4
"National" music: 30
Nature, musical impressions of: 29
National romanticism: 79
National Zeitung: 90
Newman, Ernest: 40, 91, 156
Newmarch, Rosa: 40, 91, 99, 186
New York Philharmonic Orchestra: 130, 155
Niemann, Walter: 186

Nikisch, Artur: 85, 90
Norfolk Festival: 125ff.
Norway: 107
Novacek, Victor: 88
Nurminen, R.: 176
Nurmio: 175
Nya Pressen: 13
Nyland Student Corporation: 18,
    19n.

Ohqvist: 179
Oksanen: 177
Omar Khayyam: 99
Orchestra: Helsinki, 15, 16n., 64,
    67, 134, 135; Berlin Philharmon-
    ic, 21, 85; Scala, 90; Lamoureux,
    91; Boston Symphony, 130; New
    York Philharmonic, 130, 155;
    Augusteo, 145
Oslo: 68, 134
Overtones: 55

Pacius, Fredrik: 29
Päivälehti: 32
Palestrina: 148
Pan Slavic policy: 107
Paris: 68, 91, 122
Paris Exposition: 67
"Paris Tour of Philharmonic Or-
    chestra": 67
Pastoral moods: 73
Patriotic demonstrations: 64
Paul, Adolf: 19, 33, 56, 69, 171,
    172, 178
Peer Gynt Suite: 92
Pélleas et Mélisande: 92, 119
Petrograd: 93
Philharmonic Society: 38
Pictures, living: 65
Pohjola: 47n.
Postal Manifest: 32n.
"Practical School of Composition":
    12

Prague: 68
Press Pension Fund: 64
Procopé, Hjalmar: 91, 172, 178, 184
Psychological terminology: 60

Quartet, Joachim: 20
Queen's Hall: 144

Racial idiom: 29
Rapallo: 68
Recitation with music: 81
Return of the Native, The
    (Hardy): cited, 108
Reuter: 175
Rhapsodies: Hungarian, 29; Fin-
    nish, 30
Richter, Hans: 23
Riga: 107
Ringbom, Nils-Eric: 187
Ritter: 181
Roiha Eino: 111, 151, 187
Romance of my Parents: 27–28
Romanticism: 80
Romanticism of nature: 79
Rome: 145
Rondo of the Waves: 135
Rotterdam: 68
Royal Philharmonic Society: 93, 99
Runeberg: 27, 83, 174, 175, 176,
    178, 179, 180, 182, 183, 184
Runic singers: 35
Runic songs: 80
Russian decrees: 32
Rydberg: 64, 81, 174, 175, 176, 178,
    180, 182, 184, 185

Saari: 45
Sääksmäki: 6, 7, 10
Sarajevo: 131
Sario, S.: 176
Saint-Saëns, Camille: 125
Scala Orchestra: 90
Schantz, Filip von: 29f.

Index

Scheveningen: 108

Schiller, Friedrich von: 177

Schneevoigt, George: 134

Schönberg, Arnold: 128

Schubert, Franz: 27

Schybergson, G.: 175

Shakespeare, William: 158, 172

Sibbe: 4

Sibelius, Aino (Järnefelt): 23, 37

Sibelius, Christian: 5, 8, 142

Sibelius, Christian Gustav: 4

Sibelius, Johan: 4

Sibelius, Johann Julius Christian
(Jean), *life:* birth, 4; genealogy,
4; nationality, 4; childhood environment, 5; musical talent, 5;
family, 5; mother, 5; childhood,
6; first piano lessons, 6; love of
nature, 6, 10, 73; sense of reality,
7; reader, 7; first composition, 8;
chamber music, 8; knowledge of
instruments, 9; Grieg influence,
9, 13; creative urge, 10; passes
examinations, 10; studies law,
11; enrolls at Academy, 11;
studies with Czillag, 11; studies
with Wegelius, 11f.; preference
for violin, 12; debut as composer, 13; friendship with Busoni, 14; onesidedness in musical
education, 16; first meeting with
Flodin, 17; receives scholarship,
18; first trip abroad, 19; impressions of Berlin, 19; attitude to
Wagner, 20; return to Finland,
22; engaged, 23; goes to Vienna,
23; introduction to Brahms, 23;
introduction to Richter, 23; introduction to Fuchs, 23; works
with Goldmark, 23; studies orchestration, 24; first orchestral
work, 26; sketch of Kullervo
Symphony, 27; appearance and
character, 28; patriotism, 32;
performance of Kullervo Symphony, 35; goes to Karelia, 36;
marriage, 37; honeymoon, 37;
teaches composition and theory,
37; Kajanus' interest in him, 38;
writes *En Saga*, 42; *Creation of
Boat*, 44; attitude towards leitmotif technique, 48, 58; goes to
Italy, 53; goes to Bayreuth, 53;
gets government stipend, 54;
teaching activities, 54; goes to
Paris, 67; goes to Italy, 68; begins Second Symphony, 68; at
Heidelberg, 69; conversations
with Strauss, 70; settles in Lovisa,
70; lyrical works, 81; spiritual
transformation, 85; settles in
Tvärminne, 87; settles in Järvenpää, 87; builds house "Ainola," 88; begins Third Symphony, 88; goes to England, 90f.;
returns to Finland, 91; invitation
from Royal Philharmonic Society, 93; conversation with
Mahler, 97; conducts in Norway,
107; leaves on foreign tour, 122;
attitude towards religion, 123;
receives call to Vienna, 123; goes
to England, 124; invitation to
conduct in United States, 125;
writes *Oceanides*, 125; receives
honorary title, 129f.; goes to
United States, 129; 50th anniver-
sary, 134; civil war in Finland,
141; moves to Helsinki, 142;
letter re plans, 143; conducts in
London, 144; Scandinavian tour,
145; writes Tapiola, 155; attitude to own work, 159; influence
on contemporary music, 161
———, *works:*
All'overtura, Op. 65: 65, 163

Andantino for cello and piano, 9, 166

And I questioned then no further, Op. 17: 84, 179

At the Draw-bridge, Op. 66: 65, 164

Autumn Night, Op. 38: 84, 86, 180

Aunt Evelina's Life in Music, 81

Belshazzar's Feast, Op. 51: 91, 92, 172

Black Roses, Op. 36: 84, 179

But my bird is long in homing, Op. 36: 84, 179

Canzonetta, Op. 62a: 85, 165

Concerto in D minor for violin and orchestra, Op. 47: 88, 165

Death (Järnefelt's *Kuolema*), Op. 44: 85, 171

En Saga, Op. 9: 27, 38ff., 119, 163

Enticement, Op. 17: 83, 179

Festivo, Op. 25: 65, 163

Finlandia, Op. 26: 42, 65, 67, 90, 131, 163

Fool's Song of the Spider, Op. 27: 56, 171

Impromptus for Pianoforte, Op. 5: 82

Karelia Overture, Op. 10: 43, 163

Karelia Suite, Op. 11: 57, 82, 163

King Christian Suite, Op. 27: 56, 67, 90, 131, 171

Kullervo Symphony, Op. 7: 27, 34ff., 53, 173

Kyllikki, three lyric pieces, Op. 41: 85, 167

Legend, *The Swan of Tuonela,* Op. 22: 44f., 58, 67f., 86, 90f., 163

Legends, Op. 22: *Lemminkäinen and the Maidens,* 44, 45, 51, 54, 58, 163

Lemminkäinen in Tuonela, 6, 11, 44, 93, 163

The Return of Lemminkäinen, 44, 48ff., 67f., 93, 163

Love Song, Op. 66: 65, 164

Luonnotar, Op. 70: 82f., 124, 178

Malinconia, Op. 20: 85, 166

March Snow, Op. 36: 84, 180

Night Ride and Sunrise, Op. 55: 121, 164

Nights of Jealousy, 82, 184

On a Balcony by the Sea, Op. 38: 84, 86, 180

Oma maa, Op. 92: 142, 175

Overture in E Major, 26, 163

Pan and Echo, Op. 53: 120, 164

Pélleas et Mélisande (Incidental music), Op. 46: 92, 119, 171

Piano Quartet in C Major, 24, 25, 166

Piano Quartet in E minor, 9, 166

Piano Quintet in G minor, 22, 99, 166

Pohjola's Daughter, Op. 49: 21n., 47, 92f., 131, 164

Romance in C Major, Op. 42: 85, 165

Scaramouche, Op. 71: 124, 172

Scène, Op. 25: 65, 163

Scène de ballet; 26, 163

Scènes historiques I and II, Op. 25 and 66: 11, 42, 65, 81, 123, 163, 164

Scout March *(Jaegermarsch),* Op. 91: 141, 175

Serenades for violin and orchestra (D Major and G minor), Op. 69: 124, 165

Sigh Sedges Sigh, Op. 36: 84, 180

Snöfrid, Op. 29: 82, 185

Sonata in F Major for violin and piano, 12, 16, 166

Song of the Athenians, Op. 31: 64, 174

Spring is flying, 83, 179

Index

Spring Song, Op. 16: 43, 163

String Quartet in A minor, 13, 14, 16, 166

String Quartet in B flat Major, Op. 4: 16, 166

String Quartet in D minor, Op. 56: 98f., 127, 129, 136f., 166

Suite in A Major for violin, viola, and cello, 13, 166

Swanwhite, Op. 54: 92, 172

Symphony No. 1 in E minor, Op. 39: 55ff., 83, 90, 131, 145ff., 163

Symphony No. 2 in D Major, Op. 43: 14, 57, 68, 71ff., 145, 163

Symphony No. 3 in C Major, Op. 52: 57, 87ff., 108, 135, 138, 146, 164

Symphony No. 4 in A minor, Op. 63: 35, 57, 90, 98, 106ff., 111, 121ff., 144ff., 164

Symphony No. 5 in E flat Major, Op. 82: 5, 7, 133f., 142f., 152, 164

Symphony No. 6 in D minor, Op. 104: 5, 57, 143, 145f., 164

Symphony No. 7 in C Major, Op. 105: 57, 108, 122, 136, 143, 145f., 151f., 164

Tapiola, Op. 112: 58, 73, 112, 155f., 164

Tennis at Trianon, Op. 36: 84, 180

The Bard, Op. 64: 121ff., 164

The Boat Journey (Venematka), Op. 18: 85, 173

The Chase, Op. 66: 65, 164

The Creation of the Boat, 44, 171

The Dryads, Op. 45: 120, 126, 164

To Evening, Op. 17: 84, 179

The Ferryman's Brides, Op. 33: 82, 178

The First Kiss, Op. 37: 84, 180

The Lover, Op. 14: 85, 127, 165

The Oceanides, Op. 73: 125ff., 164

The Origin of Fire, Op. 32: 82, 174

The Tempest (incendental music), Op. 109: 158, 172

Trio in A minor, 9, 166

The Tryst, Op. 37: 84, 180

Valse triste, Op. 44: 85, 92, 152, 171

Venematka, Op. 18: 85, 173

Voces intimae, Op. 56: 98f., 127, 129, 136f., 166

Waterdrops, 7, 13, 81

Sibelius, Linda: 5, 8

Sibelius, Maria Charlotta: 4

Simellus, J. A.: 176

Singakademie: 90

Singers, runic: 35

Slav composers: 29

Snoilsky: 183

Society, Philharmonic: 38

Sola, V.: 176

Sonata, Viennese: 112

Sonck, Lars: 87

"Spirit of the Woods" (Rydberg), music to: 82

Stagnelius, E. J.: 184

Stenhammer, Wilhelm: 145

Stockholm: 68, 145

Stoeckel, Carl: 125, 129

Strauss, Johann, Jr.: 27

Strauss, Richard: 21, 70, 90

Strindberg, August: 92, 172

Student Corporation: 19n., 42

Style, Finnish: 80

Suomi (Finlandia): 65

Susman: 181

Svendsen, Johann: 30

Swanwhite: 92

Swedish Theatre: 64

Symposium: 41, 42, 56

Tableaux from the Past: 65

Tannhäuser: 20, 53

Tanzberger, Ernst: 40, 122, 187

Tapio: 155

Tavastjerna, Karl August: 33, 83, 179, 182, 183
Tavastehus: 4ff.
Tavastland, province of: 6
Teaching methods: 54
Tempo indications: 89n.
Terminology, psychological: 60
Thematic treatment: 74
Törne, Bengt von: 56, 187
Topelius: 180, 182, 185
Toscanini, Arturo: 90
Tremolo, use of: 22, 24
Trochaic metre: 121
Tryptich, Aino: 33
Tschaikovsky, Peter: 29, 72
Tuonela theme: 47
Tuonela: 46n.
Tuoni River: 93
Turku: 5n., 29
Tuulusa Commune: 87
Tvärminne: 86

University of Helsinki: 11

Väinämöinen: 21n., 91, 92n., 93, 122

Väisänen, A. O.: 31, 187
Veyola, Y.: 177
Vienna: 23
Vienna Conservatory: 123
Viennese Sonata: 112
Viborg Student Corporation: 42

Wagner, Richard: 20, 22, 52, 53, 70, 97, 161
Wakefield, Mary: 99
War, Civil: 141
Wecksell: 180
Wegelius, Martin: 11, 12f., 15f., 19f., 23, 55
Weingartner, Felix: 86, 90
Weiss: 181
Weneen luominen: 44
Wennerberg: 171
Wood, Sir Henry: 91
Wolff, Hermann: 70

Yale University: 130f.

Zillag, C.: 11